COLLECTOR'S GUIDE TO
DECOYS

Wallace-Homestead Collector's Guide™ Series

Harry L. Rinker, Series Editor

COLLECTOR'S GUIDE TO
DECOYS

LINDA AND GENE KANGAS

Wallace-Homestead Collector's Guide™ Series

Wallace-Homestead Book Company
Radnor, Pennsylvania

Copyright © 1992 by Linda and Gene Kangas
All Rights Reserved
Published in Radnor, Pennsylvania 19089, by Wallace-Homestead,
a division of Chilton Book Company

Designed by Anthony Jacobson
Manufactured in the United States of America

Library of Congress Cataloging-in-Publication Data
Kangas, Linda.
    Collector's guide to decoys/Linda and Gene Kangas.
        p.   cm.—(Wallace-Homestead collector's guide series)
    Includes bibliographical references and index.
    ISBN 0-87069-614-9 (hc)—ISBN 0-87069-580-0 (pb)
        1. Decoys (Hunting)—Collectors and collecting—United States.
    2. Decoys (Hunting)—United States. I. Kangas, Gene. II. Title.
    III. Series.
NK9712.K37   1992
745.593′6′075—dc20   91-50679
                                                      CIP

1 2 3 4 5 6 7 8 9 0 1   0 9 8 7 6 5 4 3 2

My Decoys

Here they lie in silence,
Battle scarred and worn;
Never again to feel the touch of waves,
Their days of deceiving duty over.

They had no choice but to do,
The whims of man their creator;
Luring their beautiful likeness,
Down into death's row.

No more to hear the shot and shell,
Nor the hunters seeking thrill;
No more to feel the icy waters,
Nor early morning chill.

They lie here in my collection,
Their final resting place;
Weather worn and weary,
Cracked wood and faded paint.

Together in my daydreams,
Returning to days of past;
We will search and seek their likeness,
And the sound of wings beating fast.

—Ron Olson, 1986

Contents

Acknowledgments

It was a great pleasure for us to be invited by Harry Rinker to write *Collector's Guide to Decoys* for this popular Wallace-Homestead series. Harry, Kathy Conover, and Troy Vozzella of Wallace-Homestead Book Company have made this project memorable for us.

We perceive this publication to be the *Handbook* for beginning collectors, although career collectors will find the extensive listing of museums a first-time compilation. So, to provide an extensive source guide, we requested information from many knowledgeable people from each flyway and hunting region. Our heartfelt thanks go to Ron Olson for his original poem ''My Decoys,'' Steven Vernon for directing us to patent research, and a host of good friends for specialized regional information: Roger Barton, Paul Brisco, Dean Dashner, Henry Fleckenstein, Charles Frank, Bernie Gates, Merle Glick, Gary Guyette, Nicholas Kondon, James Mc-Cleery, Dick McIntyre, Jackson Parker, Ron and Janet Sharp, Bob Shaw, Hal Sorenson, Bud Ward,

Porter Hopkins, Frank Schmidt and Jamie Stalker. They provided the names of museums, auction houses, restorers, and undervalued carvers from their areas.

We greatly appreciate the efforts of the staff at the Ward Foundation for providing information leading to our introduction to the modern wildfowl carvers portrayed in this volume and those at the institutions included in the museum listing for graciously providing information about their collections.

Thanks go to the auction houses who have always supported our efforts in publishing decoy lore: Richard A. Bourne, James Julia and Gary Guyette, Inc., Richard W. Oliver Gallery, Decoys Unlimited/ Ted Harmon, and Garth's Auction's, Inc.

A lot of folks willingly supplied photos or allowed us access to their collections. Without their carvings, this book would not be as instructional. It is a general attitude of sharing which permeates this collecting field. We thank you all!

COLLECTOR'S GUIDE TO
DECOYS

Introduction

Since purchasing our first decoy over two decades ago, we have learned much and gained valuable insights through first-hand experience with over one hundred thousand decoys. These hands-on experiences form the basis for the information in this book.

When anyone first begins to develop his own collection of decoys (or any other collectible), many important questions soon arise. Where can you go to find decoys? How do you learn to evaluate them? What are they worth? How do you decide what to collect? What about fakes? Where can you meet other collectors? Which museums have collections on display? What do you do when you attend your first auction? What else should you know?

This book attempts to answer these basic questions and offer advice to beginners. Accompanying the text are hundreds of photographs and many illustrations to help familiarize you with the variety of regional decoy styles in existence across North America. The different styles offer a choice in the direction of collecting. In addition, fine examples of miniatures, shorebirds, non-working carvings by known decoy makers and more recent decorative wildfowl sculptures are included to demonstrate the range of additional collecting possible. Individualized collections of merit can be built once collectors become aware of their own personal preferences.

Perhaps you already own one or more decoys or waterfowl carvings and would like to learn more about them. This book should point you in the right direction, assist you in your collecting persuits, and help you avoid some of the pitfalls common to most collecting fields. Twenty years of active involvement with decoys are reflected here for your benefit, and we will be happy to continue to be of assistance to you (see Appendix G for our address).

Collecting is fun and educational. New friends can be made. It is never too late to start.

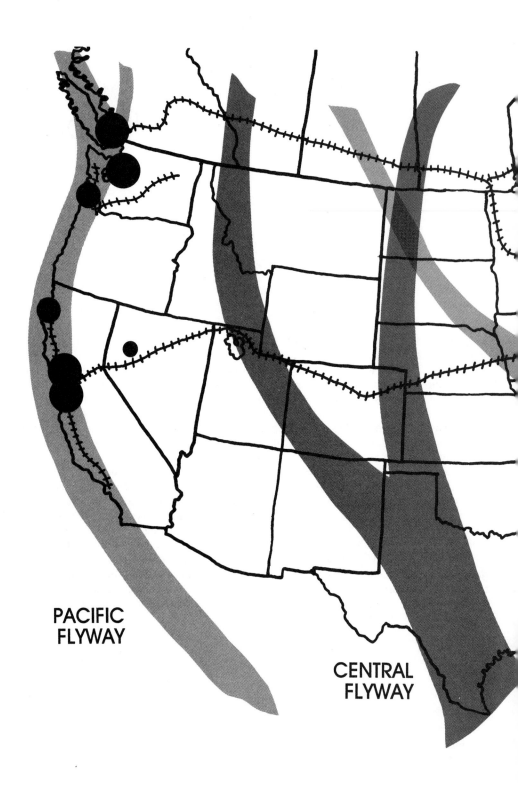

PACIFIC
FLYWAY

CENTRAL
FLYWAY

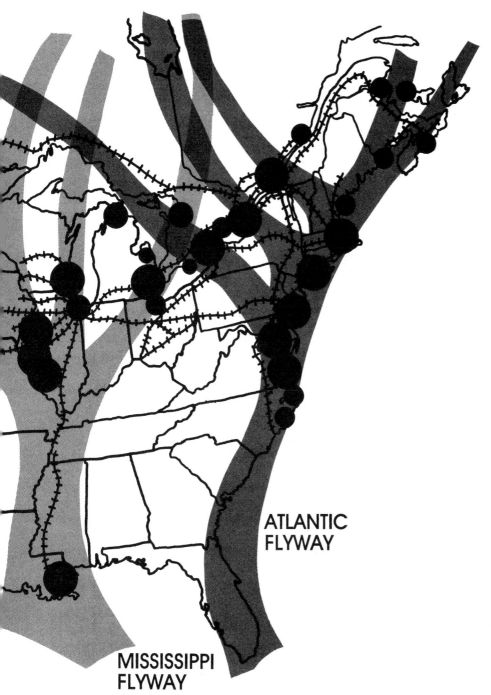

ATLANTIC
FLYWAY

MISSISSIPPI
FLYWAY

Most decoys were made in the thirty to forty years following 1875. The demand for waterfowl coupled with the expansion of the railroads produced the great but short-lived market hunting era of North America. This map shows the waterfowl migration flyways as well as the major hunting regions at the end of the 19th century. The railroad lines shown (circa 1885) were used by market gunners to ship birds to the nearest city market.

CHAPTER ONE

Developing a Collecting Philosophy

In the old days of decoy collecting some thirty to sixty years ago (many of our good friends were collecting then—lucky them), some people were able to accumulate hundreds, even thousands, of decoys. Pickings were easy and relatively inexpensive. One Chicago collector told us he would drive through Wisconsin on weekends to look for decoys. He wouldn't pay more than a dollar each and then only for Masons in original paint. He was able to fill his station wagon on each trip. Others bought decoys of all sorts and in all conditions. They bought whatever caught their eye, or whatever quantity of ducks they had to purchase just to get the few they really wanted. Back then, it was much easier to acquire small groups or entire rigs. They came from hunters and their families, carvers, shops, shanties, and were even found beached after big storms. Inexpensive decoys were plentiful. Some early collector/dealers such as William Mackey and John Hillman constantly bought *and sold*, usually keeping the very best for their private stock. Others mostly bought and kept.

Such mature collections, after twenty to thirty years of being carefully edited and selected, contained many superb lures authored by both distinguished known and superlative unknown carvers. With such a variety to choose from, it was inevitable that quality collections could be easily built—collecting decoys was in its infancy and competition was limited. Today, finding good decoys and building a fine collection might appear nearly impossible. However, anyone can do it and at any price level.

Quality or Quantity?

Many believe that when they have limited extra money to spend, they can only afford medium to low quality decoys. These folks often buy a decoy whenever they get $50, $100 or $200 together. At auctions or shows they tend to acquire several decoys with their money, and their collection grows numerically. When you have a limited amount of money, what is the best way to spend it? Do you buy six or eight mediocre decoys or one or two well-chosen carvings in excellent condition? How do you make this decision? First, take the time to think about what you like and look for that type of decoy. If the type you like is out of your current price range, save your money until you have enough to buy it. Why? Because the better bird will have an appreciation value not possible with the lesser decoy. It is better to build a fine collection slowly, with forethought and planning, than to throw one together by purchasing every decoy you see at your local flea market or antiques show or whenever you have spare money. This does not mean, however, that the highest priced decoys are necessarily *good* or the *best* decoys. These terms are subjective and every collector must decide what they mean to him.

Developing an educated point of view and a game plan will result in a better collection.

If you want just one or two decoys around the house or office and don't plan to spend over $100, then any waterfowl carving which strikes your fancy will be fine. If you want more than a couple of ducks and are willing and able to spend several hundred dollars for each, then you should consider buying good decoys of quality *and* value.

Building a Better Collection

What Are Good Decoys?

They are the better works by a particular carver. If by an unknown maker, the same applies—they are fine representations of a particular hunting region's style. Decoys produced by one maker over his entire carving career are not usually all the same quality level. Very early birds may illustrate an evolving style; those from later in a career often display a decreasing proficiency. Good birds from a particular carver usually spring from the time when he is regularly producing in a strong personal style, and often great decoys come from such periods. Another consideration is that some carvers, such as Chincoteague hunter Ira Hudson, made different price grades to accommodate buyers.

The most desirable decoys are almost always in original paint by the maker, and in decent body condition. It is these which will most likely retain at least the purchase price if bought at market value.

Lastly, a good decoy should increase in value over the years.

How can you find out if a decoy is a good example of a carver's work and is in pretty good original condition? It's easy, but it takes time to learn. Buy books and catalogs and study them, go to shows and auctions to window shop—you know, look but don't buy—and, finally, become friends with knowledgeable and honest folks in the field.

Find Out What You Like

Through studying, shopping around, and occasionally buying something you like, you begin making some decisions. Do you like one or two species of duck better than others, or all of them? Does one particular carver's work or region's styling attract your eye? Do you gravitate toward birds in near unused condition, or those which evidence life on the water and under the gun? Do you like stickups or floaters? Do you prefer cork, wood, paper, or metal construction? Factory or handmade decoys? Nineteenth-century or twentieth-century birds?

Presently, collectors accumulate what is in or around their own territory so that most collections of Michigan decoys or Louisiana lures or California birds are found in those very states. On the east coast, collections fre-

Top: Curlew, Cobb family, Virginia. Middle: Tern, unknown maker. Bottom: Mallard hen by Caines brothers, South Carolina.

quently contain birds from several of the coastal hunting spots, often combining those from Maine, Massachusetts, Connecticut, New Jersey, Virginia, the Carolinas and so on. Some folks prefer to concentrate on the works of just one carver whose decoys they admire greatly. Mini-collections of one maker's work within a larger, more varied collection also have been formed. Certain species are the collecting criteria for others, such as an accumulation of only goldeneyes or mergansers.

Miniatures. Due to space limitations or simply an eye for the jewels, some acquire only miniature carvings. Small wooden models of larger working decoys represent an interesting group

of collectibles. They generally range in size from one to three inches. Because miniatures usually exist in excellent condition, it is possible to know approximately what larger, well-worn decoys looked like when first produced. Miniatures can also be used to help identify rare or previously unknown works by known carvers. Collections of working decoys and their tiny companions could be one focus of a collecting direction. You could also look for miniature decoys by famous makers of full-size versions. Regional representations and species accumulations are certainly possible. Little carvings typically reflect not only the maker's normal style but also the style common to the region where they originated. A

Miniatures. Grouping of various species by Elmer Crowell, Harwich, Massachusetts.

Miniatures. Mallard pair by Charles Perdew, Henry, Illinois.

Miniatures. Pairs of wood ducks, American mergansers and goldeneyes by George Boyd, Seabrook, New Hampshire.

Miniatures. Merganser pair by Doug Jester, Chincoteague Island, Virginia.

Miniatures. Canada goose and scoter by Joseph Lincoln, Accord, Massachusetts.

Decorative. Walking mallard drake by Ira Hudson, Chincoteague Island, Virginia.

few of many known decoy craftsmen who also whittled desirable miniatures include George Boyd of New Hampshire, Doug Jester of Virginia, John Rider of Ohio, Charles Perdew of Illinois and Horace Crandall of California. The miniatures of each of these carvers are as different as their working decoys and flyway locations.

Miniatures generally cost less than decoys by the same carver. They are sometimes actually rarer. Being small makes them fairly easy to display and take care of. They are readily transportable, sturdy, in demand and perhaps undervalued. Some represent the carver's best work.

Decoratives. Besides producing miniatures, many decoy makers also created full-sized

Decorative. Half-bodied flying mallard by Chauncey Wheeler, Alexandria Bay, New York.

Decorative. Flying mallard drake by Gus Wilson, South Portland, Maine.

Decorative. Wood duck by Charles Hart, Gloucester, Massachusetts.

non-working waterfowl sculptures. The restrictive limitations of their functional designs were of much less concern when they began experimenting with elaborate waterfowl portraits. Elements too fragile for a decoy could enhance a decorative. For that reason, many have longer tails, extended necks, open wings and more detailed and complex paint patterns. Carvers such as Ira Hudson of Chincoteague, Virginia, considered his decoratives to be his top-of-the-line carvings. When selling, he charged the most for these works. Decorative carvings make interesting additions to decoy collections because they help illustrate the aesthetic range and capabilities of each maker. Decoratives also are cross-over pieces which fit comfortably into folk art and/or antiques collections.

As you begin to collect and study the entire range of a carver's career, you will more than likely have some contact with both decoratives and miniatures. Whether you choose to

Decorative. Rising mallard drake by the Ward Brothers, Crisfield, Maryland.

Decorative. Standing wood duck by Orel LeBoeuf, St. Anicet, Quebec, Canada.

collect them or not, you can certainly learn considerably more about each maker. Take a closer look the next time some are available and find out more about them.

Define Your Collection

By making decisions about what you really like, you can concentrate your efforts of study, time and money. As a result of your focused efforts, your developing collection will automatically become a better collection. A better collection usually is not a static entity.

Keep in mind that decision making for every collector should be an ongoing process. The first several years of education should help establish a direction of interest. Following that might be a time of refinement or expansion. Smaller collections within the larger might be cultivated. New areas can be discovered and embarked upon. Tangent study collections of weights, keels, patents, or hunting paraphernalia could expand historical interest.

Be sure to think about how you will finance your hobby. Few people can afford to support a full-fledged growing collection from the household budget. Some collectors buy more than they want to keep when the opportunity arises, and sell later at a profit. This goes into the collection kitty. Important decisions will have to be made concerning when to let things go that you previously bought.

It isn't necessary or even wise to keep

everything forever. A collection is more than an accumulation. It is the gathering together of a group of interesting items to be studied and appreciated by the collector and others. In its development, there should be accessioning and deaccessioning. A mature collecting attitude allows one to decide when decoys no longer fit the present collection. *Edit*. This also helps provide extra finances necessary to apply to the purchase of the next desired decoy. Buy the best you can get for the money you have. Save money. Be patient. Make decisions. Upgrade.

Doing Business With Friends

Let's break away for just a moment to think about friendship. It is almost certain that in every collecting area friendship is misunderstood by novices. The scenario is always the same. A newcomer and a veteran collector come together. Each is enthusiastic—the newcomer wants to learn and the veteran wants to teach. And so for a time, whether it is months or years, they pal around together, discuss the merits of decoys at shows and upcoming auctions, pore over reference materials, and generally have a good time. The newcomer is always learning. Now, this relationship is inherently a good one, enjoyable and profitable to both parties.

Then a glitch develops. It may be the tutor's fault for not teaching his friend about friendship in collecting and/or the other's never having learned how true friends behave in all situations. Whichever, there comes a time when the new collector, now armed with knowledge and experience gained from his association with his expert friend, *breeches the friendship*. This is done in any number of ways. It usually boils down to failing to share information with his friend and thereby gaining a decoy in which he knew the other had a strong interest. The expert educated the new collector and the new collector used that knowledge *against* the best interests of his friend. The friendship might disintegrate after the trust has been violated.

How can this situation be avoided? It needs to be discussed before it ever comes close to happening. The seasoned collector should instigate the exchange of views with his friend on this unfortunately all too common occurrence and together figure a way in which they can avert it.

The most important aspect of comradeship is always to keep in mind that *friendship is more important than material objects*. Keep the companionship open and forthright. It is natural that occasionally there will be certain decoys that both of you will want because the newcomer may have developed somewhat similar tastes to his friend and tutor. In conversations together try to be open and determine who has the stronger desire for the decoy. Each should give his reasons why. In deference, one will usually turn his attention to something else. Each time the two want the same bird, some give and take must take place, each one placing the friendship as his most important goal.

CHAPTER TWO

Construction Techniques and Materials

As you visit decoy shows or auctions, you will probably notice people picking up decoys and rotating them in their hands as they visually inspect and feel the textured carvings. Why do you think they do this? How heavy, light, large, or small a particular decoy is may affect its desirability. Turning the lure around helps familiarize you with its variety of components.

In simple terms, working decoys were constructed with two basic anatomical elements: a head and a body. The majority were carved from wood but other materials such as fabric, metal, plastic, papier-mâché, cork, and rubber were also utilized. Pine was the most common wood chosen for carving heads while cedar represents the most widely preferred body material. Other woods were also used, the selection being determined by either the carver's personal preference, his economics, or local availability of material. In some areas, regional woods such as southern tupelo or western redwood were the basis for decoys. You eventually might use wood type as one of your clues to identifying the origins of a decoy.

Handmade Decoys

In addition to selecting the proper and perhaps most economical or convenient wood, decoy carvers typically established particular designs of size, body position, detail (or lack thereof), paint styles, and fabrication techniques. The cumulative product of these factors became known as regional styling. In each region, the work of at least one major carver is now considered to be the classic model for that area.

Some of these recognized regional classic styles were made by Elmer Crowell and Joseph Lincoln from Massachusetts, Gus Wilson from Maine, John Blair from the Delaware River area, Mitchel LaFrance from Louisiana, Richard Ludwig Jansen from California, Benjamin Schmidt from Michigan, George Warin from Toronto, and Orel LeBoeuf from Quebec, to name just a few.

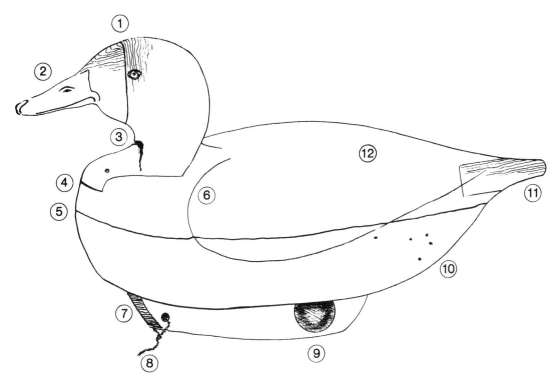

Basic decoy anatomy is similar across the continent. However, specific construction techniques, body parts, and terminology vary by region.

1. Two-piece head and neck. Anatomical parts are sometimes constructed from more than one piece of wood. This may be done to utilize the strength and direction of wood grain.

2. Bill detailing. Bills were carved with varying realistic details such as nostrils, nails (bill tip), mandible separations, and/or bill and head separations.

3. Cracks. Irregular lines usually represent cracks or breaks as opposed to construction laminations. Cracks run parallel to the direction of wood grain.

4. Neck Joint. This one is inletted or set into a carved space in the body. Other methods include flat surface to surface fits (the most common), dovetailed connections, recessed body sockets, and pegs fitting into drilled holes.

5. Body seam. Decoys were sometimes constructed from more than one piece of wood or cork. A seam line identified the lamination point or points. It does not necessarily occur in the middle. This may have been done to permit hollowing for lightness, to increase thickness, or to add strength.

6. Carved wings. Some decoys have wing outlines carved in relief from the body block.

7. Keel. To add stability in rough waters, keels of various types were sometimes added. The designs were often locally popular and may now help in identifying makers or regions.

8. Tie. Lines or tethers connected the body to an anchor to prevent decoys from drifting away.

9. Ballast weight. Many different types of weights and materials have been used over the years. The purpose of weighting was to prevent decoys from turning over in rough water conditions. Weights were also used to correct or maintain proper floating characteristics.

10. Shot marks. Small dark holes usually indicate that the decoy has been hit by stray shot. Metal pellets can usually be found at the bottom of these tiny holes. The presence of shot does not necessarily indicate age.

11. Inletted tail. Decoys constructed from soft materials such as cork or balsa wood sometimes had harder woods added for strength. This might also have been to facilitate later repairs or resulted because of a personal interest in craftsmanship and detailing.

12. Body. Decoy bodies vary in size and shape according to species, maker, interpretations, hunting methods, availability of material and regional styles.

Head Construction

Pine has been the most popular wood chosen for carving decoy heads. It is relatively easy to sculpt and detail. Historically, it was easily obtained. Decoy makers often started with an assortment of head patterns. These were thin head profiles cut from flat cardboard, tin, paper, or wood. These were mostly personal designs. The outlines of these patterns were then traced onto thicker wood for rough cutting into heads. At this point, the direction and strength of the wood grain were considered and perhaps integrated into the design. From there, the head could be refined using various sharp cutting tools. Usually each head became a recognizable species portrait.

Head construction includes consideration of the ultimate attachment method of neck and body; type of eyes, if any; and any other lifelike characteristics. The most common methods of fastening heads to bodies were nailing and glueing from the top, running screws up through the body into the bottom of the neck, doweling, dovetailing, and insetting or any combination of these. Since the decoy

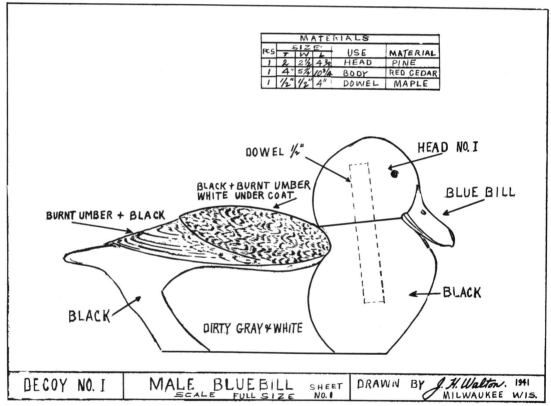

W.P.A. (Work Progress Administration) decoy patterns such as this were sold through the Milwaukee Public Museum. In the 1920s, the museum staff (mainly Warren Dettman) originated the style of decoys now referred to as the Milwaukee school. Patterns designed by Dettman were used to make decoys for his own hunting and to assist in gathering wildfowl specimens for the museum. In the 1930s these patterns were used by W.P.A. workers throughout Wisconsin. They bore a "W.P.A." stamp on the bottom. J. H. Walton, a museum employee, drew blueprints of all the patterns and offered them for sale through well-known department stores. These patterns, such as the bluebill drake shown here, reflect the style and perhaps origin of decoys commonly associated with the Milwaukee area.

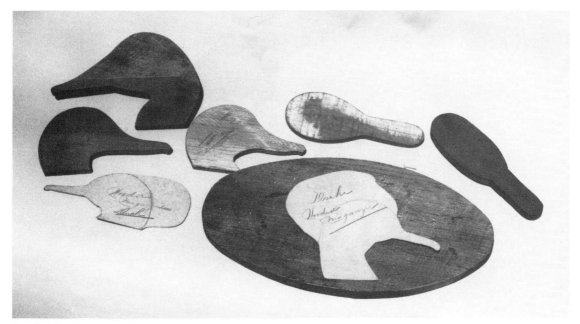

Ivar Fernlund paper and wood head patterns.

was a frequently used tool, it was necessary that it withstand wear and be repairable. Therefore, the head/body joint needed to be carefully planned. Strength was important. Construction techniques and other details evident on a decoy are very likely evidence of regional origins and perhaps the maker's identity. For example, noted maker Gus Wilson of Maine almost always inletted heads into bodies with large bold neck seats. He also detailed his heads with oval shaped carved eyes and stylized carving on the bottom side of each bill. While the large inletted neck seat is historically a typical Maine feature, Wilson's specific bill and eye detailing are easily identified with him.

In other areas, different procedures were practiced. The Cobb family of Virginia sought out curved strong branches and roots from which to shape animated necks and heads. They also selected hard durable oak for bills. Obviously, strength and serviceability were important to them. On Prince Edward Island in the Canadian Maritimes, geese and brant lures

often had heads fabricated in two pieces with the joint line running vertically through the middle of the head. By doing so, the wood grain intentionally ran vertically up and down to protect the long thin necks and was directionally changed to horizontal for the bill. Shorebird carvers frequently inserted sturdy metal nails into their decoys to represent thin, delicate bills. Examples of many other ingenious solutions exist.

Some carvers sold or gave heads to others who carved their own bodies, assembled the two and painted them themselves or perhaps had a third party paint them. Each person did what he felt capable of doing to his own satisfaction. If someone else made better heads at a reasonable price, carvers bought or bartered for them. Most painted their own decoys; however, if there was a renowned decoy painter in the area and a hunter wanted his birds to have that particular finish, he would hire that painter.

For instance, Ben Schmidt heads have been found on Victor bodies painted by

A George Boyd finished plover and body block.

Body Construction

Schmidt. Perhaps someone in a hurry for a rig brought headless bodies to Schmidt for refurbishing. It is well-known that Ben and his brother Frank joined body parts made by either of them in the making of decoys. John English heads are familiar on William Quinn bodies. Mrs. Edna Perdew painted decoys made by numerous Illinois River carvers. Decoys abound to visually testify to the involvement of more than one person in their making.

Body Construction

Since the decoy's body was to work in water, it was important that it be seaworthy, moisture resistant, reuseable, repairable, and have proper floatation characteristics. Cedar proved to popularly fulfill these general requirements. Two basic body types exist; solid and hollow.

Decoys were hollowed to lighten them, thus affecting how they floated. This also made large numbers easier to carry or transport. Several variations of hollowing techniques were employed. In one method, two or more pieces of wood were temporarily assembled, carved on the exterior, disassembled, hollowed on the interior, and then permanently reassembled. Body joints or assembly seams typically run horizontal to the water and above the decoy's waterline. Decoys used along the Illinois River exemplify this type of construction. By contrast, hollow decoys from the St.

Sam Denny black duck with body profile pattern.

D. W. Nichol teal showing various stages of completion.

Clair Flats, like those by Thomas Chambers, were lightened by carving in from a flat bottom which was then covered with a watertight, thin bottom board. Nate Quillen was a nineteenth-century boat builder and cabinet maker from that region who used the bottom board technique on some of his decoys. Other examples of his were hollowed in a very different, unique, and probably tedious manner. Quillen drilled a long horizontal hole into the body starting in the rump area below the tail. Then, with the aid of a specially designed, long-handled, curved knife blade, he meticulously whittled away at the interior through the small, round access hole. When completed, the hole was caulked, plugged, and sanded smooth. The body style of these painstakingly hollowed decoys is now referred to as "boat shaped" and is quite different from the more traditional flat-bottomed types.

A few east coast makers hollowed their wooden lures from the top by cutting larger access sections in the decoy's back and then resealing or covering the opening. This kept seams well above the waterline. Sometimes openings were covered with flexible materials such as sheets of canvas or tin. Watertight seals were maintained with applications of white lead, tar, or an assortment of other nautical adhesives.

Bottom identification. Rare ballast weight marked "A. Nichol S.F."

Weights

Because decoys were designed to simulate the floatation of live waterfowl, added amounts of ballast helped regulate the wood's bouyancy. Throughout the years, all types of ballast were experimented with and used. Early on, rocks fastened with cords worked. All types of metal items such as chains, horse or ox shoes, railroad spikes, bolts, and rods counterbalanced decoys. Lead, however, became the most popular ballast because of its weight and workability. The designs of weighting systems may be of some value when trying to determine a decoy's origins, since certain methods remained constant over a period of years. Some makers uniquely individualized their weights, some signed them, and others produced them commercially. Flat-bottomed twentieth-century decoys from Michigan often have wooden keels weighted with lead; Crisfield, Maryland decoys don't. Birds from Ontario's Prince Edward County are sometimes characterized by weights that hang and swing below the lure on two bent wires. Large old swan decoys from Maryland can be found with heavy removable keels.

Tool Marks

Every carver was a woodworker. He not only maintained his own set of tools, but he also developed procedures for using them. Closely studying numerous examples of a maker's efforts should begin to help familiarize you with recurring trademarks. Styles might change but tool marks or evidence of process often remained constant over a career. When the same tools are used, the resulting marks can be measured and analyzed to potentially identify the divergent works of a particular maker. Indepth studies of one maker or family can provide documentation of the typi-

Two Views of hollow decoys.

Back view of Sam Hutchings goldeneye illustrating carved checkered textures to reduce glare and suggest feathering.

cal surface marks and measurements one might expect to find. Students of an individual maker's works will be able to itemize such consistencies.

The work of Davey Nichol of Smiths Falls, Ontario, illustrates such a study. Two small holes can almost always be found on the bottom of his lures. These indicate his method of attaching a temporary wooden block used to secure the lure in a vise or clamp while carving. These holes are small in diameter, consistently spaced less than two inches apart, and were plugged with wood after carving was complete. Other Nichol marks include a consistent diameter and endgrain texture of a head attachment screw hole plug; mechanical coggle marks on some heads near the bill; the

tendency of wing tips to vary in height and length from left to right; slight angling of tails; and the size and character of painted comb markings. One of Nichol's painting techniques was to repeat the same color from one bird to the next. His brush marks and combing are also distinctive. A more complete and accurate compilation of such individual studies drawn from many serious researchers would provide a more systematic written analysis of decoy styles for future student study.

Tool marks might also be helpful in differentiating the works of two similar carvers. For example, if a person decided to copy or follow the style of a recognized local trendsetter, he could not duplicate all of the tool marks unless he possessed exactly the same tools and used

William Pepper bluebill head, body and removable inletted bill.

them in an identical manner. A right-handed person copying the work of a left-handed person would undoubtedly make some subtle changes or adjustments. An accurate knowledge of tool marks might prove helpful in detecting counterfeits.

Factory-Made Decoys

A great demand for tasty waterfowl meat in late nineteenth-century restaurants and marketplaces encouraged the dynamic growth of an already existing grass roots activity. Those who once only hunted for their families and neighbors now spent more of their time on the water and in the marshes and fields shooting hundreds and even thousands of ducks, geese, and shorebirds each year for the market. For nearly fifty years between 1870 and 1918, hunting waterfowl as well as other fish and game for market provided a steady and important income for many American families. As these hunters needed more guns, ammunition, *and decoys*, the total community economy benefited.

Coinciding with this, shooting for sport by the rich and sometimes famous also developed and helped expand commerce. From about 1850, wherever there were concentrations of waterfowl, hunting lodges were built and exclusive clubs were established on privately owned marshes. The movers and shakers of business and politics were often members of more than one club in different parts of the country where they traveled for in-season sport throughout the year. Their activities spawned the need for club managers, guides, *and decoys*. Their needs also helped build business for transportation companies such as passenger railroads and ships to get them to their destinations; weapons and ammunition for their shooting; special sporting clothing, hunting dogs, *and decoys*.

Therefore, as early as the 1870s, individual carvers began to manufacture decoys on a commercial basis, often setting up a business in their own back yard workshops.

Three methods of framing: (1) Wire frame for stretching canvas, (2) bent wood frame for stretching canvas, (3) cut wood for nailing slats.

Some of the earliest factory establishments were started by now famous names in decoy annals: George Peterson (1873–1884), Detroit Michigan; Harvey A. Stevens (ca. 1880–1894), Weedsport, New York; J. N. Dodge Decoy Company (1884–1894), Detroit, Michigan; Mason Decoy Company (1896–1924), Detroit, Michigan; Strater and Sohier (patented 1874), Boston, Massachusetts; W. Acme Folding Decoy (1895–1910), St. Louis, Missouri; and Animal Trap Decoy Company of America (1896–1940s), Lititz, Pennsylvania.

Many of these individuals, such as Harvey A. Stevens and Madison Mitchell, made decoys before going commercial. They simply continued in their original manner and style of carving while greatly expanding production, often requiring extra employees. Others, like William James Mason, The Herter's Company, and The Evans Duck Decoy Company, opened businesses using mass production duplication equipment. Some designed decoys which they hoped would be useful and ap-

pealing to hunters in all parts of the continent. Literature documents well over 100 decoy factories, some still in existence today.

Whether the factory utilized hand carving or lathe production techniques, the basic processes were the same. The head and body were carved separately, then attached, detail carving was added, and then the decoy was painted. Sometimes eyes and weighting systems were attached. Production makers usually made differing grades at several price levels. The simpler and less time- or material-consuming styles were at the lower end of the price structure. The more realistic decoys were purchased by wealthy clients for either their rigs or their mantels. Some individuals tapped their creativity to satisfy themselves and made elaborate, one-of-a-kind carvings. Today, these are appreciated for their rarity and artistic merits.

The Mason Decoy Factory (1896–1924), Detroit, Michigan, was the most universally known decoy factory. Founded by William James Mason, it began as a one-man operation

Branded signature "A. Elmer Crowell" (maker) and "Winthrop" (hunter/user).

Maple machine mallard body pattern by Joel Barber. Used on a duplicating lathe.

Bottom identification. Carver signature "F. Bach."

in a back yard shed at the Mason home. In a short time the demand grew and James moved his shop to larger quarters and hired help. James lived to see his business prosper and grow into larger quarters. He died in 1905 of a contracted illness and his two sons continued to run the small but successful endeavor until a series of events (including the availability of cheaper competitive hunting decoys) put an end to the business in 1924.

The Mason bodies and heads were turned on a duplicating lathe and then hand finished. Each bird was hand painted in a style recognized today as strictly Mason. Over the years, other factories and individuals emulated the body patterns and paint styling of the Mason Factory. This was a testament to the popularity of his designs. Mason produced most species of ducks and geese hunted in North America in five grades (price levels). They were, in order of quality, the Premier, Challenge, No. 1 Glass Eye, No. 2 Tack Eye, and No. 3 Painted Eye. The last three are also known as Standard or Detroit grades. In addition, Mason would accept orders for custom-made decoys, and examples of these rarer types pop up around the country. Models also changed from year to year. Early Masons do not have the same look as later Masons.

Although Mason's decoys were one of the most prolific factory products of all times, not every hunter had a good word to say about their adaptability to particular water conditions. Mason decoys were well-shaped and finely painted for each species, with rounded sides and a narrow flat bottom. On choppy or rolling waters the lures bounced around or rolled over, quite uncharacteristic of a live bird on the water. Therefore, some hunters claim they weren't much use. But sales over the years prove an overall different story, especially since these decoys were copied by those who couldn't afford to buy the real thing.

Mason Factory decoys, today, are considered one of the most desirable factory lures collected. Yet even a beginner can buy into the Mason club. Prices range from a couple hundred dollars for an original paint Standard grade model to many thousands for the best or rarest of the Premiers.

Don't limit yourself to learning about just one factory. Look at them all—there is endless variety. And, if you are buying a factory bird for your collection, buy only those in the very best original paint and condition. If you are interested in the factory aspects of this collecting field, a collection of *all* of the different factory models and related literature could be a most interesting hobby.

Undesignated Factory Decoys

Some carvers made so many decoys they could very well be classified as a factory operation even though they are not so designated by either themselves or the public. For example, Harry Shourds of New Jersey is reputed to have made tens of thousands of decoys for hunters all over America. His business was so large it helped support a railroad station in his town. Numerous Havre de Grace, Maryland, carvers, after adopting the use of the duplication process, produced thousands of working lures up to the present. These were made for sale. Shouldn't they be considered the same as a factory-made decoy?

So, what are collectors looking at as they turn decoys around in their hands? Lots! There is much to learn and the best way is to begin with first-hand experience, asking questions, and exposing yourself to the broad spectrum of existing reference material.

Patents

Decoy makers have been patenting their decoy designs and inventions for well over a century. There is no published research in this area. We spent many afternoons poring through the U.S. Patent Office *Offical Gazette* at Cleveland State University several years ago. Patents were found on designs by some well-known and some lesser-known makers. Each listing notes the patent number assigned, the category, name of patent holder, and application date. Following this is a decoy sketch and a description of the patented idea.

We have included the following information to provide additional insight into construction techniques.

The earliest patent we uncovered was "A decoy duck for sporting purposes, comprised of India Rubber. . ." applied for and granted to J. Foster of Philadelphia in 1869. Some other discoveries include:

Jacob Danz, Jr. of St. Paul, Minnesota, a known production decoy maker, held several patents. Three were found for water and stickup purposes from 1881, 1883, and 1884. There could be more by him!

Another factory, Strater and Sohier entered a patent in 1874. One of the features of their design was that "after removing the head and the float, the shells of the body portion nest together for transportation."

John Tax, famous Minnesota carver of beautifully sculpted wooden Canada and snow geese, designed and patented in 1939 a "lightweight water bird decoy comprising a painted fabric skin, comprising but five fabric sections assembled together by stitching and shaped to represent a water bird and light weight buoyant material filling the skin. . ."

Bernard E. Ohnmacht from LaFayette, Indiana noted for his 1940 patent of swivel-headed custom weighted cork decoys. Patents by others were strictly for weighting or tethering systems. Perhaps Ohnmacht considered patenting his now documented layered sealing/painting technique.

This is an interesting area of research available to anyone so inclined and with access to a library with a collection of patent books. It's something even a novice can dig right into. Nearly every state has one or more Patent Depository Libraries. Publishing the results along with the original drawings of the inventions would be an important contribution to decoy literature.

CHAPTER THREE

Collecting Old Decoys

Where to Find Decoys

Where They Used To Be

In the beginning of the collecting era, decoys were often acquired directly from the carvers or hunters who owned and used them. When collecting decoys became a national grass roots hobby in the 1960s, pickers and dealers spent long hours on the road buying up truck and car loads at a time. They would usually choose the very best decoys for themselves. The rest were then sold to friends and local antiques shops as well as at flea markets and newly developing decoy shows sponsored by fledgling decoy clubs. Yearly auctions, another new activity, also provided a commercial outlet.

During the 1960s and 1970s, everyone flocked to the decoy shows. There were at least one or two in each flyway, and they were usually held on weekends at motels with rooms, cars, and trucks filled to overflowing with every conceivable style, condition and price of decoy. Those were exciting days—friends, surprises, finds!

However, changes were afoot. By the 1970s and into the 1980s, several entrepreneurial auction houses began to organize all-decoy sales which added new energy and excitement to the entire collecting field. Enthusiasm for the shows and get togethers was high! Within a few years, though, decoys were selling for higher prices at auction than dealers or collectors could get privately. Prices lured many good decoys into the auction galleries and away from the shows, setting the stage for the slow demise of the previously energetic and interactive private sector.

Today, the market carvers are long gone and few contemporary waterfowlers continue making traditional wooden hunting decoys for use under the gun. Remaining shanties are empty as are most barn lofts. The forty-year long frenzy of a once newly discovered collectible has transported nearly all decoys from their original hunting grounds to living rooms, galleries, and auction houses. A few still wait for their discovery. So now, in the 1990s, where does one regularly find decoys to collect?

Where They Are Today

We're all in luck to a certain extent. The decoy community is quite well organized with clear pathways laid out to pursue the hobby. There is something for everyone to like and many ways to acquire. Pursuing all the sources at first is your best bet because it will help you develop an overall perspective of what exists.

Private Collections. The majority of people who seriously collect decoys will, at times, sell or trade. They can be found through collector club meetings, club membership directories, classified advertisements in trade papers, shows, and auctions. Using the list of organizations in Appendix F, join several decoy clubs both locally and distant. Some provide membership lists and newsletters. Signing up for committee work will surely help you make friends more quickly. Club committees often hold meetings in their homes where decoys are proudly displayed and discussed. Become part of the management of your region's activities and travel occasionally to others more distant.

Find out who is your closest collector neighbor. Make friends far and wide, make appointments to see collections when in other areas, keep in frequent touch by telephone and letter writing. It is *not* a breach of etiquette to be a bit socially *bold*. You may suggest to a collecting acquaintance that you will be passing through his area and would very much like to see his collection. Decoy people usually welcome serious interest and they are at ease replying that it will or will not be a good time for them. Use this approach in person or by telephone. Most will be gracious and welcoming. You will gain a great deal.

Dealers. There are numerous part-time and full-time specialty decoy dealers who attend decoy and antiques shows, have shops, and sell through the mail. They normally advertise in the trade journals, usually offer regular shopping lists, and are most always interested in helping you add to or subtract from your collection for a fee. Contact them and sign up for their mailings. Study their decoy offerings by comparing written descriptions with pictures in books and magazines. Let the dealer know which birds you are interested in and he will send you photographs. If you are still interested, you can normally have the bird shipped to you on approval. Usually, you are required to send a check which the dealer holds in his office. The decoy is mailed to you, and you have an agreed-upon number of days in which to make a final decision whether or not to buy. If you don't like the duck, call and then return it immediately. Your check will be returned. It's very easy.

Visit dealers' shops when in their areas and be sure to stop to talk with them at every show. It is especially helpful to telephone a week or two before a show which you both will attend to see if there is anything in which you might have an interest. If so, have him take it to the show and put it aside so you can have the first chance to examine it. This is done all the time.

Shows. There are still good shows to attend most any season of the year. Use Appendix F to become acquainted with all the conventions throughout the continent. A few are strictly for ''old decoy'' collectors, but the majority are combinations of antiques, working decoy carving contests, and present-day decoratives. A few conventions have associated auctions. Decoys and wildfowl carvings are brought by carvers, collectors and dealers wishing to sell or trade. Their motel rooms are chock full of lures and related hunting paraphernalia. There is much to see, and a lot of conversation flows at these events. In fact, it is nearly impossible to see and do everything at a multifaceted show.

Myriads of activities are planned at most conventions: convention halls are often filled with sale tables or booths; cars, trucks, vans, and mobile homes parked in the lots are often open and loaded with goodies; there are carving and other contests; auctions and meetings. This is all of the *obvious* hurly-burly. Actually, it can take a very energetic and devoted collector to manage to see all that is available. Shows make great weekends!

You should realize that there are several levels functioning simultaneously at these shows. Beyond casual conversations with dealers and acquaintances and the serendipitous location of a "wonderful" carving, there is also a behind-the-scenes reality that one should discover.

Shows and auctions are often held at motels, and in that case, dealers and collectors fill their beds, dressers, TV tops and floors with things for sale. Even while some are selling in the banquet rooms, many personal rooms remain open for business. One is expected to walk the halls and enter each and every open door which leads to a room whose decor is definitely "sporting." You are encouraged, unless a sign reads "Please Do No Touch," to look at, inspect, pick up, and exclaim over every item that catches your fancy. Hold that duck and ask the owner, who is usually relaxing in a chair, to tell you about the bird. He may begin by talking about the carver or how it was made or when and where he found it. Whatever he says is information which you should store away in your mind while you examine the lure. Pick up another one and ask another question. Visit other rooms and meet people, inquire, examine, and compare. This way, you might discover items of interest which you had never seen before. You will learn things about original paint versus repaint, repairs, restorations, what to expect on different carver's decoys and other invaluable information. Ask questions and *listen* to the answers.

Then, in the evenings after the business of the day is done and dinner has been enjoyed, folks often gather in each others' motel rooms to relax and share stories and jokes. It is during these social times that one learns what the old days were like, how someone made a big find, what's coming up at the next auction, where to get your decoy fixed, and so on. To be invited, ask one of the "old-timers" where to go for an evening. You might knock on an open door, introduce yourself to those in attendance and ask if you may join them for awhile. Sit down, on the floor if necessary, and *listen*. The talk will flow around you.

There are numerous other related shows such as gun, sporting, and antiques to which dealers often bring decoys. And, too, regional collectors get together for swap and sell picnics and such. Club newsletters and word of mouth will inform you of these. In many ways broaden your acquaintances, strengthen them, and share equally with people. Do not wait until the next event to renew conversations. Enjoy your new cohorts. Give and take.

Auction Houses. Several auction businesses specialize in decoys and employ experts. Check Appendix E for the names and addresses of a number of nationally recognized businesses which sell decoys regularly. Those who specialize are so noted. Their catalogs and the decoys they sell are a valuable reference source of information and learning which no novice should pass up. They should become a part of your growing library. In fact, auctions keep a constant supply of decoy catalogs to purchase and study. Write or call each firm and ask to be put on their mailing lists. Several months prior to an auction, they will send you a flier illustrating a sampling of upcoming decoys and announcing the price of the catalog. Order a catalog even if you think you can't get to the auction. Several weeks after the auction, you will automatically be mailed an after-auction price sheet listing the gaveled price of each lot. You can also order older copies for previously held auctions. Find out which copies are still available. Out-of-print catalogs can often be purchased from specialty book dealers. Chapter Six, Understanding Auctions, offers you advice on attending auctions in your first few years of collecting.

You can utilize many avenues to meet people and find decoys. There are also general antiques auctions which occasionally include a few decoys. The focus of these sales is usually Americana, or furniture and paintings, or whatever. These are held every day across the country, and the only way to find out about them is to read the trade papers carefully as well as local or regional newspapers. You probably won't be able to tell if you want a bird from one of these auctions unless you go look at it in person (they are usually not pictured or described in ads and there may be no catalog). Antiques shows still occasionally have a few nice birds. Flea markets usually contain junk birds unless a specialty decoy dealer has a booth or an unknown treasure sits waiting to be discovered. Get there first.

What To Collect

There are so many species of waterfowl lures; so many locations where they were used, each with its own styling; so many carvers, factories and time periods, that you really should consider focusing your thoughts, time and finances. Your collection will be the better for having been carefully planned, so *define* your short and long term objectives. Collect in one or a combination of the following areas, for example.

Regional. There are collections of decoys highlighting the different waterfowling regions of which there are about twenty. Often folks collect decoys which were made and used in the area they live in because the decoys are nearby and are somewhat easy to find. There have been magnificent large or small collections of the restful Delaware River region, smooth-lined New Jersey, sculptural Massachusetts, Quebec, California, Michigan, painterly Illinois and graceful Louisiana decoys to name just a few. The general waterfowling regions of North America are described and pictured separately in this book (see Regional Photo Essay). By studying each area, it becomes evident that certain styles of carving are predominant. Learning what pleases you is an interesting and valuable process.

Carvers. Within each region there were as few as several dozen or as many as several hundred decoy carvers, each with a personal style or technique which made his decoys distinct from his neighbors or hunting partners. Some collectors concentrate their efforts on one or two carver's works that they admire. One might collect the work of Robert Elliston or Charles Perdew of Illinois; Mitchel LaFrance or the Vizier family of Louisiana; Elmer Crowell, Joseph Lincoln, or Charles Hart of Massachusetts; or Thomas Chambers, Ken Anger or the Nichol family of Ontario. There were numerous carvers on the waterfowl-rich island of Chincoteague, Virginia. One might collect any decoys made on the island, or only those made by the extremely innovative and productive Ira Hudson, or the later work of Miles Hancock. Entire books have been dedicated to each region highlighting known carvers' works in pictures and text. Read them. Magazine articles report on lesser known or recently studied carvers. *Your choice of concentration could be unique in the field.* Whatever it is, be sure you are captivated and excited.

Some collectors specialize in the work of one carver, such as these by Ken Anger.

Tin factory shorebirds, foldable and stackable, in their own storage box.

Factories often made different price grades.

Factories. Over 100 factories have produced decoys since the 1870s and some are still in business. Each of these businesses produced distinctive birds destined to be used across the continent. Most are wooden ducks, geese and shorebirds; but other materials such as paper, cork, Styrofoam, plastic and cloth were used and included various bird species such as crows and owls. The Mason Decoy Factory of Detroit, Michigan, which went out of business in 1924, was one of several that made different grades (price ranges) for each species. So, you could conceivably collect only Mason Premier grade lures in all species, or Mason Challenge Grade divers, or Mason Standard Grade glass eye hens. This approach limits potential acquisitions, but creates a direction and makes collecting more challenging.

Species. Others pin their primary interest on one species of waterfowl. There are approximately thirty odd species of waterfowl hunted in North America. One Georgia doctor studied shorebirds. A Michigan advertising man has several hundred goldeneyes. A Massachusetts realtor specialized in eiders and scoters. A Minnesota investor once had hundreds of canvasbacks. Some collect what they hunt.

Songbirds are just one type of decorative wildfowl carving collected today.

What to Ask and Know

When you begin to collect, you become a student again. Ask questions, but be sure to follow up the responses with some research of your own so that your next inquiries are better-informed. When others see you are asking questions beyond a superficial level, they will come to respect you and be even more welcoming. You need to learn what characteristics reflect the region where a bird was made and who hand carved and/or painted it. "Are *all* Illinois River decoys hollow?" "What woods were used for Louisiana decoys to make them so lightweight?" "Why are many far northeastern birds unweighted?"

You need to become familiar with decoy body surfaces to accurately discern the types of surface distress birds may display. "Where were these birds used?" "How were they used and for how long?" "How does the wear on this old nineteenth-century Chesapeake lure differ from the recently manufactured wear on this replica?" Questions that start with "Tell me what you know about. . ." or "What do you think about. . .?" usually elicit an enjoyable discussion.

Pick up unfamiliar birds and take the time to see what can be observed. Ask the owner about the weighting system used by the carver and how it may be different or similar to those of other carvers. Teach yourself to look for and ask questions about repairs, takedowns, repaints, touchups and replacements. Ask people their opinions about how these affect value. Learn relative market values (see Chapter Four) so that you can respond to an offer. Keep abreast of auction sales and discuss the results with others. Ask their opinions about the condition of birds. Ask why one decoy brought such a high price, or such a low one.

Listen to discussions and observe how people do business. Ask advice. Most enjoy giving advice to others who are truly interested in hearing us talk. Soon you may be privy to the underworkings and be clued into more productive acquiring techniques.

Clues to Trading, Buying, and Selling

The extent to which dedicated and longtime collectors and dealers will go to obtain what they desire is practically limitless. You've heard stories of the unscrupulous individuals who hire helicopters to swipe weathervanes right off barn rooftops. At the same time, there are plenty of honest ways to obtain what one craves without resorting to such extreme or clandestine activities. Simple approaches sometimes work just fine, so do innovative ones. Like the fellow back in the 1970s who went out and bought an $8,000 automobile to trade for a decoy he desperately wanted. Well, anyway, that's the story.

When Money Can't Buy It

Sometimes money itself doesn't make half a trade. There was once a collector who had long been trying to convince a fellow to sell a fine decoy. One day he offered him $900 for the duck. ''Well,'' the decoy owner drawled, ''I guess not. I don't really need the money.'' Disappointed again the collector queried, ''What do you need?'' ''Nothin' much . . . but . . . I've been thinkin' about looking for another motor for my boat.'' A few days later the man returned with a new motor and headed home with the decoy. So, if you're in business for yourself or work for a business, what might you have to trade? A refrigerator? Carpeting? Plumbing? You get the idea.

Collectors often encounter people whom they think might have odd or unusual atti-

tudes. Like the people who are not collectors but are somehow attached to their decoys with an unseen umbilical cord. Others just don't see any reason to make changes, even little changes, like parting with an object they have out in the garage or down in the cellar. Then there are those who are afraid to sell anything for fear they will get taken on the price even if they are offered full or more than full market value. These people are legion! Trying to buy from them can be extremely frustrating. What can you do? *Think*! This is the fun of collecting. Resort to ingenuity and quick thinking, even if it takes a year or more to figure out. Others have done it.

One logically-minded collector persuaded a hunter to accept brand new, light-weight plastic factory decoys in trade for his old, worn heavy wooden decoys. Both were delighted! Contemporary carvers have fashioned new wooden gunning decoys in trade for a hunter's older collectible rig. This is a good deal for both since the hunter didn't have to bother with seasonal refurbishing to have bright attractive lures for the following year.

Those who collect in different fields can often come to terms. Antique firearms could be traded for decoys. Even an exchange of services can bring two people together. One could provide guiding services for a top flight fishing or hunting excursion; do carpentry work on a house, hunting cabin or boat; or perform professional services such as medical, legal or dental work. Any of these could come

Decoys can add character to the corner of any room. (From the collection of Phyllis Ellison, Michigan.)

into play as one-half of a trade when a straight buy/sell transaction just won't work.

A Cleveland collector, who once worked for Remington Arms, is known to have traded shot gun shells for ducks. Well-known photographers and authors have often helped publicize and promote the works of unpublished carvers, and were sometimes compensated with rare and unusual decoys for their time and expertise.

When It's Trade Only—A Decoy For A Decoy

Some of us have spent months or years looking for that very special decoy a friend wants so we can trade it for what we want. Well, we embarked on a wild goose chase over a decade ago when we naively began to search for a Mason Factory *Premier* coot. Well, there were none publically known then and still are not known. Needless to say, that particular trade was never consumated. I do believe a few people got a chuckle when we asked after the coot. But we are optimistic that one still might be found!!

Two long-time friends tried to get together on a trade that eventually took several years. One of them was a doctor who informed his receptionist that whenever his friend was in the lobby of his office with a paper bag, she was to treat him as a high priority patient and put him in an examining room. Many decoys were compared behind closed doors, but no trade ensued. This went on until the right bird was found, and the friend knew it! He went to the doctor's office, left his bag, but didn't stay this time. The doctor called him on the telephone and simply said, "You got me!"

Sometimes more than one decoy or a decoy and cash are combined to make the trade closer to even in value. In some trades each owner identifies what he thinks is the top retail value on his decoy. Then one says to the other, "If my teal is worth $550 and your merganser is worth $500, I need $50 cash plus your bird to make this work." Well, that might hold true if each of you paid $550 and $500 respectively for your decoys. But, what if each owner had under $200 invested in his bird? Since each very much wants the other's, a simple decoy for a decoy trade would make the best sense. *It is not always necessary to obtain the last dollar value in a trade where both parties are getting fairly equal trade value and are quite happy with the merchandise.* Most values change and are subjective anyway. Getting the last dollar value should not be a prerequisite to completing a deal.

Remember you need to meet people, see their collections, and "talk ducks" in order to know what others have, and what they still want. The trade papers are filled with classified buy/sell/trade ads purchased by those who want to expand their reach. If you have a computer, begin a file.

How To Afford Collecting

There are many ways to generate money while actively collecting. In fact, for many years our collecting activities actually supported our growing collection. The collection had its own income-generating bank account.

Early on, it was possible for many collectors to buy large groups of similar decoys or rigs for very reasonable prices. They would then keep what they liked best and sell or trade off the rest, always for more money than they had invested. This, then, returned the money spent and added decoys and more money with which to purchase again. Sometimes just a few decoys are bought, one or two kept and the extras hopefully sold for a profit. When buying low, one should always be able to sell for more. Unless you use one collector's humorous policy of "buy high, sell low and make your profit on volume!"

It usually makes sense, when deciding how much to spend on a purchase, to buy on the low side of market value because when you ultimately resell you are more likely to receive more than you initially paid. This should be true for both short and long-term sales plans, and would allow you to reinvest in more or higher quality items.

Use your personal abilities and services to assist you in acquiring whatever you want. In

A unique way to display decoys (Ellison collection).

the decoy world there is, continually, a lot of trading and swapping. Make many friends, establish a social network and be open in your desire to trade decoys or services for decoys.

Let Everyone Know

Subtly slip the subject of decoys into everyday conversations with your non-collecting friends. At parties, one collector used to begin conversations with "I'll listen to stories about your mother if you'll listen to stories about my decoys." Word of mouth is a strong advertisement which could pay off now or later. Let collecting acquaintances know what you are looking for, and keep them updated. Occasionally advertise "Looking For Decoys" in your local newspapers. Advertise in decoy newspapers and magazines to buy or sell. Don't be a closet collector!

Buy Now, Sell Later

Whenever the opportunity arises, acquire a duplicate of what you are purchasing for yourself. This allows you to trade the double for something else you want. Always look at new and exciting lures. One of the better ways to improve a collection is to *upgrade*. Buy a better example of a decoy you have and then sell the old one. And, while you are thinking and studying, don't be afraid to entertain the idea of changing the direction of your collection. Sure, it is wise to work toward short and long term goals, but be flexible enough to change your direction when you see a more exciting path. Perhaps you spent three years collecting Evans Factory decoys and now Stevens captures your fantasy. Either keep the Evans and move on to Stevens, or sell the Evans to finance the new move. As you grow and learn in the field, keep looking at your decoys individually and as a personal grouping. Continue to shape and develop it as your collecting eye becomes educated and your tastes become more personalized. Design a collection of distinction!

Quality First

As discussed in Chapter One, Developing a Collecting Philosophy, decide what types of decoys you want to look for at the present time. If you like the sturdy qualities of twentieth-century Michigan lures, choose a carver whose work you respond to. If a top shelf quality Ben Schmidt redhead in excellent original or mint paint and condition is going for $975, don't buy a repainted canvasback of his with a replaced bill for $150 just because you only have the $150 at the time. Again, *save your money until you have enough to buy one, better decoy.*

Investment Vs. Pleasure

Some think buying decoys for investment is akin to any number of other social travesties. To them, "for investment" diminishes the heart and soul of collecting "for the love of it." Forget that nonsense! Money is being spent. Everyone of us can have a darn good time in this hobby even as our decoys increase in value, planned or unplanned. And many of us plan for an increase.

If purchasing with investment in mind, you should buy what you like, preferably below present market value. At that point, you are already ahead of the commercial value. When reselling, be certain the time is right for the particular decoy you wish to sell. Decide whether a private or public sale will be better and determine which auction house and which sale might be most advantageous. Get advice.

Personal pleasure has little to do with common market values. You can pay in excess of present norms for personal reasons—perhaps the decoy fills a special niche in your collection and makes it better, maybe you got a bargain recently and paying a little more for the next bird just balances the scales of commercial value, perhaps one special decoy actually raises the value of your whole collection, or maybe you just like it.

The most important thing to remember about being a collector is to *like what you acquire*. Then, whatever the economics, your life will continue to be enriched.

CHAPTER FOUR

How to Value Decoys

Most people equate value with dollars and cents. However, value actually has several different meanings. Value equals historical significance, cultural reference, archaeological importance, personal nostalgia and/or commercial merit. To the person interested in any one of these particular considerations, that value often supercedes the other categories. *Value*, therefore, is viewed by individuals in various ways and is most often a subjective term.

Root head merganser made circa 1790 to 1810 and attributed to Roger Williams of Long Island.

Historical Value

You've probably heard the phrase "George Washington slept here." Historical events and the people normally associated with them are part of the complex nature of our country's growth. Any item that can be identified with that development may be historically valuable. This includes decoys owned by famous North Americans, regional decoy design prototypes, early pre-contact native decoys, and very early examples by contemporary Americans.

Many decoys were branded by their makers and by the hunters who used them.

President Grover Cleveland was an avid duck hunter and shot over a rig of decoys now associated with him. A Cleveland decoy in almost any condition certainly retains its historical value from several perspectives. So do lures marked with the names of well-known sailing vessels. Decoys like these would be welcome additions to collections of sailing memorabilia, presidential profiles, and sporting history. Specific dollar values are difficult to assign to such items.

Cultural Value

As immigrants began feeding their families, the decoy was quickly adopted as a valuable tool. The earliest decoys made by these new citizens, therefore, also have significance. They help explain the transformation of the ephemeral native lure into a more permanent object. Decoys such as those attributed to Roger Williams of Sheepshead Bay, Long Island, certainly fit this category. By recent standards, their circa 1790–1810 dating is earlier than any other known non-native decoy. What value should be placed on the decoy(s) of the first carver in an area to develop what might be considered the classic or prototypical design of the region? Commercially, Roger Williams decoys have sold for much less than artifacts made one hundred years or more later. Sales prices do not necessarily reflect values in a noncommercial context.

The settlers, coming from culturally diversified countries, introduced their varied traditions, religious beliefs, trades, crafts and arts to Canada and America. The study of the comingling and merging of this continent's divergent cultures throughout the centuries is a

Rendering of an early Indian stuffed skin decoy wrapped with reeds.

fascinating and relevant study. Decoys were an important facet in the food chain of this complex developing continent. Decoys, as tools used to obtain food, were fashioned by the dictates of each settlement's new environs and their cultural heritages.

The flamboyant and colorful lures of Louisiana, the elaborately carved birds of Quebec, and the Puritan-influenced styling of Connecti-

41

cut and early Ohio decoys illuminate each area's predominant "old country" influence in the new country. Painting styles such as those found on imported Scandinavian or German furniture and accessories appear also on decoys in those settled regions. The cultural value of preserving decoys' integrity and longevity as one aspect in the study of the continent's melange is important.

Drawing of two thousand-year-old native decoy found in Nevada.

Archaeological Value

Native decoys found by archaeologists in Lovelock Cave, Nevada, in 1924 provided us with considerable information about the nomadic culture that designed and used them. These artifacts also helped to establish the evolution of the decoy from idea to implement in North America over two thousand years ago. What dollar value can or should be placed on one of these bundled tule and feather canvasbacks? They are irreplaceable. Until earlier decoys are discovered, the Lovelock decoys remain the ancestral heritage of all other wildfowl decoys made throughout the history of North America.

Nostalgic Value

By the same token, decoys that possess a strong personal appeal also have very subjective values. How could you place an accurate dollar amount on a decoy made by your grandfather? Perhaps the two of you hunted together for many years until he was no longer able. He retired his decoys, giving you one in remembrance of your good times together. How much is that duck worth? How could you sell it?

There are numerous reasons for strong personal attachment to any particular item. Maybe it was your first decoy, maybe it was a present, maybe there were special circumstances associated with your acquiring it, or maybe you just simply love it. Attempting to establish rational monetary values under such emotional influences is probably impossible. Buying and selling are difficult at best. Personal pleasures and lasting satisfaction are also valuable commodities.

Commercial Value

Decoy buying and selling is business. Like any business, items are exchanged for profit.

Profits are realized by advertising, good timing, wise buying and dealer reputation.

Mallard drake by the George Peterson decoy company which was in business from 1873 to 1884.

Prices vary with changes in trends, fluctuations in the economy and availability of items to be sold. As of 1991, the highest price paid publicly for a decoy at auction was $319,000 for a preening pintail drake by Elmer Crowell of Massachusetts. That is the extreme and certainly does not reflect the norm.

Typically, the rarest examples in their best original condition command the highest prices for each maker. That does not, however, mean that values for all makers are equal. Market conditions vary continuously with some regions dominating sales activities for particular periods of time. Massachusetts decoys were hot for a while. Then those from Virginia and the Carolinas received much attention. Good decoys from areas such as the Upper Chesapeake Bay of Maryland, Michigan and the Maritimes sold for considerably less at the same time that other areas were more popular. Collectors should develop a broad perspective of all offerings.

To understand the reality of dollars spent on actual decoys, let's take a look at several examples. As stated, a special Elmer Crowell pintail sold for $319,000. Remember it was a special decoy in a special time period and there were special circumstances. No other Crowell decoy has come near to approaching that level. More typical Crowells normally realize auction amounts between $1,000 and $5,000 per decoy. That is a far cry from $319,000. Some "beater" Crowells or those in poor condition sell for as little as $100. Anyone owning a Crowell and seeing the news of a record sale usually gets delusions of grandeur and assumes it is another treasure. Values of decoys by all makers vary considerably. It is difficult, if not impossible, to be specific about prices without a knowledge of the marketplace and a first-hand examination of a particular decoy.

A person attending a decoy auction watched an Orel Leboeuf bluebill decoy sell for $1,000. He approached the underbidder and offered him another LeBoeuf bluebill for the same price. The underbidder purchased the decoy for that price because it wasn't a common bluebill, it was actually the only known bufflehead and in mint condition. The underbidder was lucky he didn't win the bluebill at auction as he wouldn't have been offered the second. The seller of the bufflehead hadn't done his homework but was pleased with what he thought was a top price even when informed of the species. Both parties were happy.

Pricing Trends

The best examples of most things generally appreciate in value over the years. Here are a few examples. A Harry V. Shourds Canada goose purchased in 1971 for $150 sold in 1986 for $4,000. Mason Decoy Factory standard grade decoys used to be priced around $25 in the early 1970s and by the late 1980s mint examples were selling for $1,000 or more. North Carolina battery decoys were not highly sought after in the 1960s. Many were sold for a few dollars. By the 1990s, however, an aggressive group of collectors steadily pushed prices to four and five figures for many of them. That's a good example of supply and demand. When the same thing develops in other areas, prices rise correspondingly. Observant collectors might be able to make profitable acquisitions before prices rise and then sell when they reach a level of desirable profitability. Of course, we all don't collect for profit, but it's nice to know that lures purchased with your hard-earned dollars continue to appreciate in value.

Every year record auction prices are realized for different makers. Publicity from these events helps draw out previously unknown decoys. High prices also persuade collectors to cash in some of their prize possessions. Remember, there is a right time to buy and a right time to sell.

The Market Today

The decoy market went through a leveling of prices across the board in the late 1980s after it reached unparalleled heights in 1986. It was in 1986 that the most decoys were sold at auction to date, prices for decoys exceeded $100,000 several times, excitement and expectation were at their greatest, and all major decoy auction houses were selling enforce! The next few years, from 1987 through 1989, saw a staggered economy. International unrest caused consumers to be more cautious and many held on to their cash instead of investing in stocks or art. During that period, high-end lures dropped dramatically; only a handful of decoys sold for over $50,000 publicly and none sold for over $100,000. Excellent quality, medium priced decoys valued between $3,000 and $8,000 managed to hold their value. The very moderately priced ($150 to $2,000) decoys were soft. But, collectors did not lose their passion and dealers and auction houses recovered.

Fortunately, the last decade of the twentieth century began with a sharp upturn in decoy economics. According to noted auction reviewer Jackson Parker writing in *Decoy Magazine*, the strong increase of the 1990s proved to be the second highest grossing auction year with $6,074,911 gross profits compared to the astounding $7,166,938 of 1986. A few statistics can show how confident buyers became in 1990. In 1986, 98 decoys sold publicly for more than $10,000. In no other year from 1981 to 1989 did more than 55 sell for over $10,000. In 1990, 106 birds sold for more than $10,000. Additionally, 1990 had the highest average price per lot sold ever, at $1,271 per. Mid-level decoy prices went from healthy to robust, and the lower range strengthened.

The decoy field, with its infinite collecting choices, has its share of buying trends. Ward Brothers decoys were hot in the 1970s. Massachusetts carvers such as Elmer Crowell and Joseph Lincoln were very popular in the late 1970s and early 1980s, as were shorebirds of all kinds. For years, New England decoys accounted for a great number of the decoys bought and sold publicly and probably privately as well. But the late 1980s saw a great surge of interest in Canadian decoys, especially those from Ontario. And, decoys from Virginia and the Carolinas have grabbed publicity as southern collectors vie heatedly for regional rarities.

The 1990s will see other areas and carvers discovered. Waterfowling decoys from Quebec, the Maritimes, Louisiana, Michigan, and the west coast are among the next potentially hot collecting areas. Today, they remain a collector's paradise with thousands of exciting, historical artifacts at usually reasonable prices. Unpublicized carvers from the more popular areas may also be a good investment for both satisfaction and value.

CHAPTER FIVE

Undervalued Decoys

In every collecting genre, there are the recognized masters and masterpieces to which great monetary value is firmly attached. As well, wonderful items of excellent quality and beauty are actively bought and sold at more reasonable, but still pricey, levels. In the decoy world, many birds have achieved a high level of popularity not only because of their excellence but also due to their availability (Elmer Crowell and Ira Hudson made tens of thousands of carvings) Popularity and a higher price tag are also achieved when decoys receive substantial publicity through word of mouth, exhibitions, catalogs, books and magazines, and public sales.

There were literally thousands upon thousands of waterfowlers throughout North America, and many decoys by gifted carvers have yet to draw the attention of collectors outside their particular hunting region. Because these carvers have not yet received national attention, their values may not have begun to climb or yet reached their peak.

Because many decoys by known makers are still in original paint and excellent body condition and can be bought privately and at auction for moderate prices, it seems a good idea to highlight some of them here. This will allow collectors to quickly key in on affordable lures of merit. We have chosen a few carvers from each region, all of whom made working decoys. Some also carved decoratives and miniatures. The majority of birds produced by them can still be purchased for under $1,000. Works by most of these carvers can be found in decoy books documenting their particular regions (see Appendix C).

The Northeast

Maritime Provinces

John Smith (1882–1968), Sherose Island, Shelburne County, Nova Scotia. While not the most artistic decoys in Nova Scotia from the folk art standpoint, Smith's decoys were well developed and finished and are historically important. He was by far the most productive maker of the region and had widespread influence. His decoys, or decoys patterned after his, have been found from Yarmouth to Cape Breton Island. He also carved smaller decorative decoys and other items. **$25–75**

Prince Edward Island. The sculptural brant and geese decoys from P.E.I. are some of the most unusually active representations of working waterfowl carvings. The geese and brant were often made with two legs to be thrust into the shore rather than designed as floaters. In these northern waters, the hunters must have observed great grooming activities as they emulated the birds far-reaching necks plucking and smoothing feathers on chests, stomachs and over and under raised wings. If these decoys had been made on the Virginia or Carolina coasts, they would be bringing tens of thousands of dollars each because of the strong interest by collectors in their region's best. Many of them still bring less than **$1,000**.

Quebec

Hercule Laviolette (1903–1963), Valleyfield. Laviolette made classic Valleyfield-style decoys patterned after his uncle Henri Laviolette. They are quite detailed in the feather carving and paint work. His high quality and output have made his work very desirable. **$275–800**

Adelard Ouimet (1900–1975), St. Anicet. Ouimet's decoys are slightly undersized for the region but have nicely carved wing and tail feathers. He was a prolific carver and made all the locally hunted species as well as miniatures. **$75–300**

Robin Brothers (Decoy factory producing between 1920 and 1945), Montreal. The Robin Brothers main business was the making of shoe lasts with a secondary interest in decoys. They made several different models including hollow, solid cedar, and balsa decoys. In the 1920s, they sold them for $12 to $36 per dozen depending on quality of paint and the finishing details. Their work is interesting for its quality and variety. Well-known local carver Archie McDonald was employed by them. **$100–700**

Evariste Savage (1887–1973), Valleyfield. Savage is known for his detailed feather and tail carving in the Valleyfield manner. He made two quite distinct styles and was an influential style setter in the region. He made quality decoys without wide exposure. **$250–650**

Massachusetts

Arthur Bamford (1864–1938), Marblehead. Bamford was a taxidermist and boatbuilder, both occupations adding to his abilities as a fine carver. His heads and bodies are well-shaped, a bit oversized, but of a distinctive style. Several of his decoys are at the Peabody Museum in Salem (see *Decoy Magazine*, Sept./Oct. 1989, page 26). None have ever been offered at auction, but they would probably sell for between **$400–800**.

James Bowden (1849–1910), Marblehead. Bowden was a cabinetmaker whose furniture is much desired among the local antiques dealers. He made of rig of scoters. Hunters say that scoters flew over all the rigs to land among Bowden's decoys. Good style but most have seen much use and are repainted. Local collectors treasure them for their form and mystique. None have sold at auction, but prices range from **$100–1,000**.

Vermont

George H. Bacon (1861–1925). Bacon is probably Vermont's most famous carver because his goldeneye served as a model for Mason's rare special-order goldeneyes. See the book *Decoys of Lake Champlain* by Harrell. His goldeneyes bring a few hundred dollars, more or less, depending upon condition.

Frank Owens (circa 1850). Owens' birds were made very early, are rare to find today, and possess a fine sculptural styling. **$300–500**

Miniatures

The best known miniaturist is **Elmer Crowell** of Cape Cod who made thousands of miniatures, so many and so varied that his later "minis," which are marked with a rectangular brand on the undersides of their round bases, are suspect, possibly made with the help of his son, Cleon, and others, or even worse, imitations. Crowell's early minis were either unmarked, signed, or had a circular stamp on the undersides of their bases. The early minis, especially shore birds, sell for up to $2000, although some can be found for **under $1,000**. The later minis sell for under **$1,000** apiece, except for shorebirds which may bring **$1,000** or more.

George Boyd of Seabrook, New Hampshire and **Joe Lincoln** of Accord, Massachusetts made miniature decoys which bring over $1,000 each, unless flawed. The jewel-like minis of **A. J. King** of Rhode Island are half the size of Crowell's and twice as detailed; they've recently reached the **$2,000 to $3,000 range**.

Under $1,000 apiece, we have the excellent minis of **Morse, Gilley, Gibbs** and **Blackstone**. Robert Morse and Wendell Gilley lived near each other in Maine; Morse in Ellsworth and Gilley in Northeast Harbor, about 20 miles away. Morse's minis are of wildfowl standing on signed driftwood bases. Gilley's are so much like Morse's, except for a chip-carved base signed on the underside, that it is believed he may have copied Morse. Morse's minis sell for $400 to $600, except for pairs and shorebirds which go for over $1,000 each. Gilley's sell for **$600 to $800**.

On a par with these and costing less than $400 apiece are the minis of Jess Blackstone of New Hampshire and Harold Gibbs of Rhode Island. Blackstone made mini song birds and shorebirds identified with his JB logo under their round bases; they sell in the range of $200 to $400. Gibbs made mini wildfowl which are identified by his signature under their driftwood bases; they sell for **$150 to $250**.

One more miniaturist is **Captain Gerry Smith**, an octogenarian who is still carving. He makes minis to order in the little shop behind his house in Marblehead, Massachusetts. Price is negotiable.

The Mid-Atlantic

New Jersey

Charles Wilbur (deceased), Island Heights. Made decoys in the early to mid-twentieth century. Nice, hollow decoys made earlier by Wilbur are reasonably priced. **$200–600**.

New York

Roy Conklin (1909–1967), Alexandria Bay. Conklin was a boat captain, carpenter and hunting guide on the St. Lawrence. He carved his stylish decoys for thirty years between 1930 and 1960. Roy's birds were of established regional patterns and he continued the tradition of the long-necked, alert lure. **$400–1,000 +**

Julius Mittlesteadt (1888–1957) and his son **Robert** (b. 1911), Buffalo. The Mittlesteadts worked from 1930 into the 1950s, possibly sharing the same patterns and applying paint alike. They produced beautiful and detailed painted surfaces which often remain in fine condition today. Robert estimated that approximately 250 to 350 decoys were produced. **$500–1,000 +**

The Central Atlantic

Maryland

Carroll Cleveland "Wally" Algard (1883–1959), Charlestown. Algard's decoys are a very folky Cecil County School style with a pronounced hump in the back just forward of the tail. He carved from 1920 to 1958, making decoys out of any size and kind of wood he could acquire. Hence, there is a disparate range in the length and depth of his carvings. Some rare Algard decoys still in original paint have sold for more than $1,000. **$200–800**

Captain John Glenn (1876–1954), Rock Hall. Glenn's carving style was earlier and more refined and stylish than Jess Urie's although they both were part of the Rock Hall School. Glenn carved from 1876 until the year of his death. He often carried the bill carving to the very top of the decoy's head which is distinctive enough for identification purposes. He is quite collectible today because of the variety of species he made, many of which are still available in original paint and fine condition. **$200–500**

Scott Jackson (1852–1929), Charlestown. The bulk of his decoys were carved around the turn of the century. Although considered of the Cecil County School, Susquehanna Flats, his birds are usually sleeker and more stylish in appearance than others from his area. His work is distinguished by a slightly upswept tail and nicely carved head. Jackson was one of a handful of "Flats" makers who made tiny teal decoys. **$300–600**

Madison Mitchell (b. 1901), Havre de Grace. Mitchell began both a funeral business and a decoy carving business in 1924. Sam Barnes had taught him to chop bodies, whittle heads, and sand. Until 1931, he made all his birds by hand; but then began using a dupli-cating lathe which allowed him, with the help of apprentices, to produce over 50,000 decoys over the years. Although fitting the definition of a factory, he seems never to be listed as such in historical writings. **$250–1,000+**

Captain Jesse Urie (1901–1978), Rock Hall. Captain Jesse was one of the most prolific members of the Rock Hall School of carvers, yet he did not make thousands of decoys. The fact that he made many different species adds appeal to today's collectors. His birds are nicely carved, well-made, sturdy decoys with excellent paint patterns and colors. He worked between 1940 until shortly before his death. Many of his decoys remain in original paint. **$100–400**

Virginia

Miles Hancock (1889–1974), Chincoteague. Hancock took sportsmen on hunts from his own houseboat for many years. He made decoys of many species including geese, brant, swan, canvasback, redhead, scaup, goldeneye, bufflehead, black duck, pintail, mallard, wigeon, green-wing teal, red breasted merganser and hooded merganser. He later included some in sleeping, preening and swimming positions. He began making his decoys about 1927 by hand-chopping with a hatchet, spokeshaving them and never sanding, as he thought they should not be finished off too smoothly. In later years, he carved miniatures including shorebirds and oyster catchers. He was probably the last true "eastern shore" decoy maker of the old school. His carving and paint methods were truly of his own design. **$200+**

Doug Jester (1876–1961), Chincoteague. Jester was born and raised on Chincoteague where he fished and hunted all his life and made decoys for sale. His hand-chopping produced a narrow body which he rounded off with a knife, resulting in a multi-faceted carved surface. Of the numerous species he carved, his mergansers have a spunky character and are easily recognized. **$400+**

The South

South Carolina

Gilbert J. Maggoni (carved from the 1950s to the 1970s), Beaufort. Quit carving in 1980 and ceased making working decoys in 1960. Maggoni is recognized as the initiator of the modern decorative carving movement. His exhibitions at the Ward Foundation's early shows (1971–1975) turned the contemporary carving element. He single-handedly "switched the gears" of America's contemporary bird carvers. From the traditional slick (nontextured) floating decoy, Maggoni set birds suspended in midair, flying with feathers so real they at first appeared to be taxidermy specimens. His traditional hollow, laminated duck and goose hunting decoys are historically and regionally significant. They are not abundant, but still available. **$300+** for working decoys.

Louisiana

Jules Frederick (1903–1980), New Orleans. Jules was a plasterer who carved most of his decoys after he had retired. His large graceful decoys were carved from cypress root gathered from the Mississippi River batture in the fall when the river was low. A cousin of George Frederick, and the son of a fine old hunter/trapper whose decoys are much prized today, Jules, like his father, seldom used glass eyes. Like many of the old Delta carvers, this was an unnecessary luxury not required to lure the birds. **$100–250**

George Frederick, Jr. (1907–1977), Davant. His decoys and those of LaFrance and Joefrau are really of a group effort. But many of Frederick's own birds were carved during the last years of his life, are still available, and may ultimately be recognized as inseparable from the joint effort of the three men. Frederick's own: **$400–700**

Dewey Pertuit (1901–1967), Raceland. Pertuit was a prolific carver and one of the few professionals who used a pattern. He carved tupelo gum with a distinctive eye groove and most distinctive weight. They are perhaps the easiest Louisiana decoys for a beginner to identify. **$100–600+**

Warren A. Seebt (1896–1972), New Orleans. Seebt's decoys are interesting for two reasons. First, he painted in a most unusual impressionistic pattern using points of color that, seen from a distance, are remarkably effective. Looking at them up close, you'd have to wonder what he was drinking. Second, most of his birds were carved from balsa wood. This wood was from the life rafts of merchant vessels sunk at the mouth of the Mississippi River by German U-boats during World War II. Carving with his friend Al Beyl, a very fine craftsman, he maintained his own unique style. **$200–400**

Anthony Spongia (1900–1983), Chalmette. Pilot town and New Orleans. Spongia was a ships' carpenter and trapper at the mouth of the Mississippi River as a young man. A river man by virtue of his formative years, he used cypress root for his decoys, drying large chunks in the ductwork of his home heating and air conditioning system. His decoys bear the rounded chine of a Louisiana lugger (a fishing boat) and his paint style makes each decoy look like a boat ready to take wing. On request, he carved a few rigs of shorebird decoys, much prized today by those fortunate enough to have requested a dozen. **$100–200**

Nich Trahan (1904–1969), Lake Arthur. Trahan's decoys are quite unique. Flat and frequently oversized, they are carved from prime tupelo gum. Paint and wood were carefully applied and crafted. He was quite prodigious, but may never have used a pattern. His mallards range in size from three quarters to one-and-a-half life-size. Few Trahans are known to be in excellent condition today. **$300–700**

Laurent Verdin, Sr. (b. 1909), Crooked Bayou Blue and Pt. au Chein. Verdin has stopped carving due to eye problems. A Houmas Indian, living a nineteenth-century lifestyle, sans electricity or running water, he is truly an *enfant de marie* (child of the swamp). His decoys sold for $1.50 just twenty odd years ago; his miniatures for 50 cents. Of course, these prices were at the dock in his little settlement, a rather long and frequently arduous journey when winter tides were low and the bayous were muddy puddles. He never used sandpaper or store-bought eyes until recently, and often remarked, "When de bird close enough to see dat', he close enough to shoot." He made many unusual songbirds, and is famous for large standing brown pelicans, pintails and mallards. **$100–200** for old working decoys.

The Midwest

Ontario

Jesse Baker (1888–1961), Brighton. There are still some Baker black ducks turning up now and then. Baker decoys vary widely in quality and style. If a good Baker black surfaces, it should be in the $200 to $300 range. A Baker teal would probably be **$450 to $600**.

Hawk Catton (1854–1933), Ridgetown. Catton was not well known personally by his contemporaries, but many had heard of him. He was a sign painter and an accomplished competition shooter. He carved many decoys for sale from about 1890 until around 1930, but there remain just a few known still in excellent condition. The birds are solid, with a compact form, snakey head and neck with a smile carved into the mandible. **$500–1,500**

Harve Davern (1864–1958), Brighton. Davern made very stylized decoys with unique patterning. These birds have a place in a folk art collection as well as a decoy collection. Bluebills and Whistlers, **$200–500**; Black Ducks **$500–1,000**.

Art Herron (1880s–1960s), Peterborough. Herron's bluebills, blacks, and whistlers are still being found from time to time; and cost $200 to $300. They are good representatives of the Peterborough area. Other species are much more difficult to find and this is reflected in the price of **$500–1,000**.

Ralph Malpage (b. 1929), London. Malpage made a well-carved decoy with a United States/Canadian style. He is in his 80s and still carving, so his birds are still inexpensive and a good buy. **$100–400**

Frank Martin (1900–1978), Windsor. Martin made turtle-back decoys with well-sculpted heads and attached wooden keels. The birds have classic profiles, fairly rough paint condition, but exude a rugged folk charm. **$100–150**

Harry Martin (1870–1938), Wallaceburg. Martin's business was insurance and real estate, but he took time off each fall to hunt. He was a legendary local market gunner who made many decoys of fine form influenced by the Warin/Chambers Toronto styling. He was a colorful character, and a reasonably prolific carver between 1895 and 1935. He made hollow and solid canvasbacks and redheads abundantly, some bluebill, and possibly teal. Collectors can find lowheads as well as birds with "attitudes". **$600–1,000 +**

Peterborough Canoe Company (production from early 1900s through 1950s), Peterborough. Some of these are still in good paint and under the money. Available at times. Buy only very good paint. **$100–350**

Carl Rankin (1921–1973), Mitchell Bay. Carved from circa 1945–50 until 1970. As a marsh manager and screen shooting guide, Rankin even worked for Henry Ford after he bought the Mud Creek Club in 1963. He made a variety of decoys; canvasbacks, mallards, redheads and black ducks are of the more plentiful. His work may have been influenced by Ken Anger of Dunville and Jim Kelson and Ralph Reghi of Detroit, but Carl used a finer hand. His decoys display great form, inletted head and neck technique, and a rasp finish to the wood. **$400–1,000**

Jack Reeves (early 1900s), Port Rowan. Until his death in 1989, Jack maintained a century old family tradition of making decoys for use on the north shore of Lake Erie. A visit to the Long Point, Port Rowan area and some luck could still turn up a J. Reeves decoy. **$300–700**

Harold Wilkins (1877–1965). Wilkins had a long life and spent much of it making decoys. He lived in several places on the continent including California, Alberta, and Ontario. Because of this, one still has a good chance of finding a Wilkins decoy. Some of these are painted with his pattern-maker's care and precision and make a nice addition to a collection. **$300–800**

Hamilton Bay. This was a small area with a large duck and human population. As a result, there is still a relatively large number of decoys available from this region. By selecting good form and paint, birds made by carvers such as **Ernie England, Chic Poyton, George Wier, Harry Glover, Clary Shaw** and others

from the Bay, a collector can still find good value and interesting examples. **$300–1,000**

Prince Edward County. County birds may present one of the last chances to buy old, good form, hollow decoys. You can still find a **Gorsline, Rundle, Bartlett** and others in the **$500 to $1,000** bracket. (In the past couple of years, the increase in value of decoys has encouraged some counterfeiting in this region. Be sure of your sources.)

Unknowns. Most serious research into Ontario decoys has been done in the last ten years. For this reason, there are still a lot of fine unidentified decoys in the province. These birds are usually much less expensive than those of equal merit by a known carver. A collector soon learns that an ugly duck is an ugly duck no matter who made it. Most collectors take a lot longer to trust their own judgment and accept a quality decoy as quality, though the carver may be unknown. When confronted with a bird he has not seen before, I have often heard a collector express interest and pleasure with the decoy and then ask the question, "Who made it?" With the reply, "I don't know," the interest and pleasure is dampened. With Ontario decoys the beginner, particularly the young beginner, can take advantage of this attitude. As years go by and research continues, the chance of Ontario unknowns becoming knowns increases as would the value in that event.

Michigan

James R. Kelson (1888–1968), Detroit. Kelson was an expert fisherman turned duck hunter. He spent his life on the waters he loved and became known as an expert guide and craftsman, making duck boats and carving duck and fish decoys. It is said that Kelson made decoys as early as 1902; but his wood and balsa lures from the 1920s through the 1960s, numbering into the thousands and made

Pintail by Miles Pirnie, Michigan.

Bluebill by Fred Allen, Illinois River.

Cree Indian twig goose, Canada.

Swan by Robert McGaw, Maryland.

Back: Canvasback by John Zachman, Michigan. *Front:* Teal by unknown maker, Ohio.

Canada goose by Joseph Lincoln, Massachusetts.

Top: Eider by unknown maker, Maine.

Bottom: Black duck by Augustus Wilson, Maine.

Shorebirds by Thomas Gelston, Long Island.

Bufflehead by Harry V. Shourds, New Jersey.

Merganser by Elmer Crowell, Massachusetts.

Old squaws by Harald Thengs, Long Island.

Mergansers by Samuel Hutchings, Ontario.

Coot by Otto Garren, Illinois.

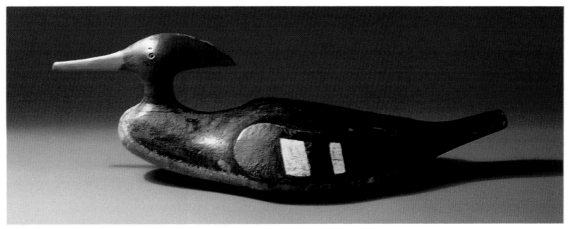

Merganser by Orran Hiltz, Nova Scotia.

Mallard by Walter Peltzer, Wisconsin.

Wigeon by Orel Leboeuf, Quebec.

with his buddy Ralph Reghi, are readily available today. The two of them developed many carving innovations. **$300–800**

Miles Pirnie (1898–1976), East Lansing. Pirnie was a biology professor at Michigan State University and a waterfowl expert. His decoys are admired and collected for their lifelike presentation of each species. Pirnie carved several hundred decoys beginning in 1935. **$200–800**

Nate Quillen (1839–1908), Rockwood. Quillen was a boat builder, decoy maker, hunting guide, locksmith and cabinet maker. He made approximately 200 decoys a year and was most productive between 1875 and 1900. He is known for his fine craftsmanship displayed eloquently in his egg-shell-hollowed decoys. His work is early, of the highest quality, and of distinctive design. No copies of Quillen's style have surfaced, most probably due to the exquisite carpentry necessary for their execution. It is to our delight that, as yet, some of his decoys still sell for **under $1,000**.

Ralph Reghi (b. 1914), Detroit. Reghi's dream was to become a professional waterfowler, and with the help of the older Jim Kelson, he stepped into that lifestyle. He developed into a master craftsman as a decoy maker and boat builder which he has continued into his later years. Friends have introduced him to contemporary carving which he has enjoyed. Reghi's decoys are bold and distinctive with stylish alertness. **$300–800**

Benjamin (1884–1968) and **Frank Schmidt** (1879–1960), Detroit. Ben's strong and bold decoys are Michigan's most well-known. His distinctive feathering technique of stamping the bird with a handmade tool rendered his birds a unique finish which is instantly recognized. (One must be cautious of imitators, though. His birds were so well-liked that other Detroit area carvers copied them.) Frank, one of his brothers and a carver himself, did his own work and also made up decoy orders with Ben for a number of years. Students of the Schmidt decoys are able to discern which birds Ben and Frank made entirely by themselves and which are half-Ben/half-Frank. Frank's early decoys are quite good and worthy of attention. Ben: **$200–1,000**, Frank: **$150–600**

Factories. Peterson, Dodge and Mason (ca. 1873–1924), Detroit. Detroit was home to several of the most popular decoy factories of the time. Most factories, as well as prolific individual carvers, made several grades of decoys with differing degrees of carving and painting depending upon their prices. For years, collectors have prized the top grades and virtually ignored the less articulated. However, there is artistic merit and pleasure for the eye in original and excellent condition lower priced factory lures. Standard grade Masons with their painted, tack, or glass eyes are often available for **$100–800**. George Peterson decoys are some of the earliest factory decoys and can be found in fine original condition at prices which have never commanded the upper ranges, **$200–800**. Jasper N. Dodge took over the Peterson shop, produced his own decoys, and has until now taken a back seat to Mason decoys allowing collectors to buy reasonably; **$250–1,000 +**

Ohio

William Enright (1913–1979), Toledo. Enright and his buddies hunted the perimeter of Lake Erie marshes with his lightweight decoys made from cork and white pine. His successful and stylish pintails are sought by collectors today. Bill entered and won ribbons at the very early carving competitions. **$200–750**

William Pepper (decoys made circa 1930s), Rocky River. Pepper made solid-bodied decoys with inletted weights in their wide flat bottoms. The most distinctive characteristic are his removable inletted bills. **$800–1,000 +**

Jack Rider (1881–1967), Port Clinton. Rider started carving circa 1900 and continued for about sixty-five years. He made several hundred ducks and geese and over one thousand miniatures. **$300–900**

Wisconsin

Evans Decoy Company (1920–1930s), Ladysmith. Evans made all of the basic species of waterfowl with nice paint patterns which fit well in a factory collection. **$200–750**

Milton Geyer (carved 1920s to present), Greenbay. He made a great lifelike bird. It has been said that many hunters sneaked up on his decoys only to find out they weren't alive. **$150–300**

Joe Gigl (1882–1962), Fremont. One of the best Wisconsin decoy painters. His mallards are special. **$150–400**

August Nelow (1882–1962), Oshkosh and Omro. Gus was a market hunter, trapper, boat builder and decoy maker all of his life. He began carving about 1900 and is reputed to have carved many thousands of decoys. Due to the numbers he originally made, there are many to be collected today. **$150–400**

Frank Resop (1875–1953), Berlin. Resop made nearly all the decoys he and his hunting pals needed (probably up to one thousand) in a folky style. **$300–500**

Frank Strey (1890–1966), Oshkosh. Strey began carving in 1910 in the basic Winnebago style. He also developed several personal styles with distinctive head carving. **$250–400**

Dewitt Wakefield (1849–1912), Fremont. One of Wisconsin's earliest decoy carvers. **$300–800**

Illinois

George Barto (1880–1959), Joliet. From 1937 to his death, Barto produced working decoys, decoratives and miniatures commercially. His decoys were hollow and painted with bold strokes and bright colors. **$250–900**

Glen Cameron (1882–1958), Chillicothe. Cameron was a professional carver and sportsman who carved approximately two hundred finely constructed decoys. He always tried to improve his birds and looked at the techniques and designs of other notable Illinois carvers. **$400–1,000+**

Walter Dawson (1882–1955), Putnam. Dawson carved thousands of decoys during his fifty productive years. A carpenter by trade, his woodworking skills turned out distinctive, well-made hollow lures. He carved different styles including sleepers and highnecks. **$300–1,000+**

Ignatius Stachowiak (1898–1964), LaSalle. Stachowiak was greatly influenced by the carving of Charles Perdew. He carved mallards, pintails, bluebill and teal decoys beginning about 1930 and continuing into the 1960s. He made about 300 birds. **$250–900**

John Stiles (b. 1908), Savannah. Stiles began carving in 1949 and continued to make handmade gunning decoys through the years. He made some decoys in a feeding position, an attractive feature to add to a collection. **$300–800**

The West

British Columbia/Washington/ Oregon

During the last twenty years, few west coast decoys have been sold publicly, so discovering values from private sales and determining those who are still affordable is difficult.

California

Richard "Fresh-Air" Janson (1872–1951), Sears Point. Janson was the west's most infamous carver, an irascible loner who for many years lived on a riverboat and carved thousands of decoys between cigarettes and drinks. His unique styling was the most influential west of the Rockies, and some of his birds are still moderately priced. **$800–1,000+**

CHAPTER SIX

Understanding Auctions

Prior to the 1960s, most decoy buying, selling, and trading was done one-on-one at the private level. In 1968 the Richard A. Bourne Company auction house of Hyannis Port, Massachusetts, held the first ever all-decoy auction; and in the next decades duck, goose, and shorebird decoys found their way into hearts and homes as both decorator items and serious collections. The mass marketing of decoys via auctions wrought many changes over the years. It has been an exciting journey, albeit not satisfying in all ways to everyone. Gradually, this once entirely casual, enjoyable hobby was transformed into a much more sobering activity. Some of the fun was gone. A decoy's worth has become a very important facet to many collectors.

In the 1960s, auctions consisted primarily of working decoys which dated from the mid-1800s up through the late twentieth century. However, decorative and miniature waterfowl carvings, as well as related sporting art and artifacts, have always been included. Eventually, thousands of North Americans were actively collecting waterfowl carvings. It didn't take long for auction catalogs to inspire interest and confidence in prospective buyers. They contained sharp black-and-white and color photographs of nearly every item to be sold, described each lot in detail, and printed estimates of the selling prices. Potential buyers have always been able to study their catalogs, usually several weeks in advance of the sales, to determine what interests them and to decide whether or not they should attend. The auction houses have developed good working relationships with their many consignors and buyers.

Decoy auctions occur throughout the year in various locations across the country. They provide collectors with a tremendous array of opportunities. Some sales contain as many as 800 decoys, and others much fewer. The major decoy auctions are frequently held in conjunction with regional decoy shows or related sporting events such as The Ward Foundation Wildlife Carving and Art Exhibition in Salisbury, Maryland and the National Antique Decoy Show in Chicago. It is advisable to order a catalog for an upcoming auction several weeks prior to the sale date so that you can casually study, review and cross reference the offerings. Do your homework. Make notes and write down questions before traveling to the auction. Now, what can be expected at decoy auctions?

Before the Bidding Starts

Dealers and collectors often set up in parking lots or motels, at or near the auction location, flea market-style to buy, sell, and swap. Make it a point to find out where this group is located and then follow up with a walk-through visit. This is a must! You might be surprised to see items similar or superior to those in the auction available for purchase out of the trunks of cars or from motel room beds. Your perspectives will be broadened! You might discover, for example, that a so-called "rare, special bird" in the auction has six almost identical rigmates out in the parking lot, or you might learn by keeping your ears open that a particular decoy is really unique and possibly a good buy. You can assimilate valuable background information or listen to astute observations; however, be advised that rumors abound. You can also meet new contacts, some of whom may become longlasting friends.

Parking lots and/or motels abound with individuals with a wide variety of expertise gleaned over many years of serious involvement. Some people are intimidated by knowledge and shy away from it. Be inquisitive, ask

Parking lot outside a decoy auction.

questions, compare notes. Most collectors are flattered and happy to share information with someone new to the hobby who is genuinely interested. Bring a couple of your own "maker unknown" decoys to show around and perhaps they'll be identified. (Caution: Don't ask for free appraisals at this time, just information.) Bring a camera. Before you even walk in the door of the auction house, you can experience and learn a great deal.

The Auction House

Get to the auction early! Some auctions attract rather large audiences, so reserving a seat is essential. Therefore, sign up for a bidding number and seat right away. Bring a comfortable cushion from home. When signing up for your bidding number, ask the auction house to put you on their mailing list. Then, throughout the year, you will receive fliers and announcements of future sales. Introduce yourself to the auctioneer and/or the specialty expert in your field of interest. Get to know them.

Preview Time

All reputable auction firms provide prospective bidders with ample preview time. Experts on the material being sold are normally present to answer your questions. At this time, you should carefully look over the offerings and determine your preferences prior to the actual bidding because many auctioneers sell in excess of sixty lots per hour. Since there is limited time to think when your item is actually

Auction under "the big top."

on the block, be prepared. Mark your choices in your catalog, know your price limitations, and determine the amount you're willing and able to pay for each choice. When the action starts, stick to your decisions.

Catalogs

Auction houses that handle better quality merchandise generally organize and sell catalogs for each separate auction. The price and quality of the catalog varies considerably by company. Country auctioneers often, at most, provide only a list in no-particular order of things to be sold. Some offer only a Xeroxed numerical list with little or no useful information. Houses that put together high quality specialty or thematic auctions provide high quality catalogs.

Catalogs should describe the terms and conditions of each sale. These include guarantees, bidding procedures, payment terms, reserves, premiums, tax regulations, estimates, shipping information, and any other special conditions. Back issues are usually available and should be considered additions to your personal library. Catalogs which include quality photographs printed on coated stock, complete descriptions of each lot, and accompanying post-auction price lists can make useful

reference tools. Leading decoy specialty houses offer this service. Many catalogs are indexed by maker. A few collectors and dealers have compiled home computer listings from all the catalogs. This facilitates their search for information regarding a particular maker, region, or decoy. Decoy catalogs normally cost in excess of twenty-five dollars each.

Guarantees. Some companies guarantee what they sell, some offer partial guarantees and others none at all. Read this section of every catalog carefully because there are potential legal implications in the carefully worded texts. Don't overlook this. The following are catalog quotations of guarantees offered by various firms who sell decoys and folk art:

Richard A. Bourne Company, Inc., Hyannis Port, Massachusetts.

". . .Catalog descriptions are guaranteed to be accurate in the matters of authenticity, condition, and measurements. Measurements are guaranteed to be accurate to within one-half inch. . .the Auctioneers will be the sole judge in the matter of refunds. All sales are final. Refunds will be given at the discretion of the Auctioneers, and requests for refunds for Lots purchased in person at the Gallery must be made before those Lots leave the Gallery. Lots purchased by Absentee bid must be examined and request for refund made immediately upon receipt of the item or items. Refunds requested on the grounds of authenticity must be made within thirty days of the date of auction, and such requests must be accompanied by at least one supporting statement in writing from an authority recognized by the Auctioneers. It is the Auctioneers' sincere intention to consider any reasonable request for a refund."

Focus: Bourne guarantees the authenticity of decoys sold as described in the catalog for thirty days from the date of the auction, and they require prompt requests for refunds for both in-person and absentee bidders.

Decoys Unlimited Auctions, West Barnstable, Massachusetts.

"All lots are sold *as is* with respect to condition and neither the Auctioneers nor their consigners make any warranties or representations, express or implied, with respect to such lots. . .the catalog descriptions are guaranteed to be accurate in matters of authenticity, genuineness, attribution, period, and origin. All sales are final except that refunds will be made on lots found to be other than described in this catalog. However, any intention of return must be expressed to the auctioneers within fourteen days after you have received your decoy. The decoys need not be returned within fourteen days but we must be notified within fourteen days of your intention to return them."

Focus: Decoys Unlimited guarantees authenticity as described within fourteen days of auction sale; however, condition is limited to the term *as is*. (As is means that no claims are made concerning a decoy's condition. Therefore, the house is not responsible for its condition, including damage or restoration.)

Garth's Auctions, Inc., Delaware, Ohio.

"*Warranty*: We guarantee the age, condition and authenticity of each item to be as represented in the catalog, or at the time of sale. Descriptions given at the time of sale take precedence over any written or prior statement. Any claims against this guarantee must be made within twenty-one days after the auction."

Focus: Garth's guarantees items including its decoys as described in the catalog for twenty-one days after the auction unless comments were made to the contrary by the auctioneer during the sale.

James Julia/Gary Guyette, Inc., West Farmington, Maine.

"The catalog descriptions are guaranteed for authenticity, condition and measurements. The auctioneers will be the sole judge in the matter of refunds.

"*Duration of Guarantee*: Request for refund for items purchased *in person* at the gallery must be made before those items leave the gallery. If you are an absentee or phone bidder and intend to request a refund for an object purchased, it must be done so *immediately upon receipt and examination of your purchases*. It is important to note that thirty-five days after the auction date all guarantees are null and void and subsequently it is of great importance that you pay for your goods in a prompt manner so your purchases can be shipped and received before the guarantee period expires."

Focus: Julia/Guyette guarantee their catalog descriptions up to thirty-five days from the date of the auction.

Oliver's Auction Gallery, Kennebunk, Maine.

". . .the catalog descriptions are guaranteed to be accurate in the matters of authenticity. . .the Auctioneers will be the sole judge in the matter of refunds. Refunds will be given at the discretion of the Auctioneers. Requests for refunds for items purchased in person at the gallery must be made before those items leave the gallery. In the case of absentee and phone bids, all guarantees on items purchased will become null and void twenty-one calendar days from the date of shipment from our gallery. **Important**: Although it is not necessary to have the merchandise in our hands within the twenty-one day period, it is necessary to contact us within that period and to notify us as to why you intend to return any item."

Focus: Oliver guarantees decoy descriptions for authenticity but not condition. A twenty-one day time period from date of shipment is set as their limit.

Sotheby's, New York, New York.

Terms of guarantee: We guarantee the authenticity of Authorship of each lot contained in this catalog on the terms and conditions set forth below.

1. *Definition of authorship*. Authorship means the identity of the creator, time period, culture, ori-

gin of the property, as the case may be, as set forth in the bold type heading of such catalog entry.

2. *Guarantee coverage*. Subject to the exclusions of (i) attributions of paintings, drawings or sculpture executed prior to 1870, and (ii) periods or dates of execution of the property, as explained in Paragraph 5 below, if within five (5) years from the date of the sale of any lot, the original purchaser of record tenders to us a purchased lot in the same condition as when sold through us, and it is established that the identification of Authorship (as defined above) of such lot set forth in the bold type heading of this catalog description of such lot (as amended by any posted notices or oral announcements during the sale) is not substantially correct based on a fair reading of the catalog including the terms of any Glossary contained herein, the sale of such lot will be rescinded and the original purchase price refunded.

Focus: Sotheby's guarantees *authorship only*, and only when listed in bold print in the caption, for five years. Attributions are not guaranteed.

Waddington, McLean & Company, Ltd., Toronto, Canada.

"Notwithstanding the previous conditions of sale, if within fourteen days after the sale of the lot, the purchaser gives notice in writing to Messrs. Waddington, McLean & Co., Ltd., that the lot sold is a deliberate forgery and within seven days after such notification, the buyer returns the same to Messrs. Waddington, McLean & Co., Ltd., in the same condition as at the time of sale and satisfied Messrs. Waddington, McLean & Co., Ltd., that considered in the light of the entry in the Catalog the lot is a deliberate forgery, then the sale of the lot will be rescinded and the purchase price of the same refunded."

Focus: Waddington, McLean & Company limit returns of decoys to fourteen days after the sale and *only* in cases where the buyer can prove a deliberate forgery.

Christie, Manson & Woods International, Inc., New York, N.Y.

"*Warranty*. Christie's warrants for a period of six (6) years from the date of sale that any article described in this catalog is not counterfeit and that any such article unqualifiedly stated to be the work of a named author or authorship is authentic. The terms "author" and "authorship" refer to the creator of the article or to the period, culture, source or origin, as the case may be, with which the creation of such article is identified in the description of the article in this catalog. Terms used in the bold type heading of each lot in this catalog, indicating the degree of authenticity of authorship, are explained in the glossary. *Any heading which is stated in the glossary to represent a qualified opinion only, is not warranteed herein. While due care is taken to insure the correctness of the supplemental material which appears below the bold type heading of each lot in this catalog, the warranty contained herein does not extend to any possible errors or omissions therein. Except as specifically provided in Christie's warranty above, each lot is sold as is and with all faults and defects therein and with all error of description.*" (From Christie's 6/22/78 sale of the Bruce Matteson collection of Illinois Duck Decoys.)

Focus: Christie's allows a six year period for questions regarding authenticity of authorship of a decoy. These must appear in bold print in the catalog. All items sold as is.

As you are now aware, a broad range of buyer protection exists. Catalogs with excellent photography, precise and detailed descriptions, along with lengthy guarantees are to the advantage of every bidder, as well as to the entire collecting field. This is an important reason why you should get to know the people with whom you are doing business.

Reserves. A reserve is the minimum price negotiated between the seller and the auction firm below which a specific item will not be sold. Some auction businesses like Garth's in Delaware, Ohio, proudly advertise that none of the lots in any of their sales have reserves. These are called unreserved auctions. It is, therefore, possible to buy considerably below estimated value or retail value if you are lucky. However, ethical auctioneers, whose responsibility is to represent the seller, will occasionally pass an unreserved lot if bidding is exceptionally low. This means that it could be withdrawn from that sale during the actual bidding process.

The purpose of a reserve should be primarily to help protect a sizeable financial investment and not merely to ensure a sale at market estimates. For instance, if the seller paid $3,000 for a decoy, most of the invested dollars might be protected by setting a reasonable reserve of $2,500. The bidding must reach $2,500 in order to be considered sold. If bidding does not reach the reserved amount, the lot is considered "bought in." This means the decoy goes back to the seller who might be required to pay a handling fee, usually in the range of five percent of the reserve. Reserved lots are generally limited to a small percentage of the auction's sale.

Reserves are commonly set near or below catalog low estimates. If reserves are not indicated in a catalog and if the catalog does not say "unreserved," personal inquiries directed to the auctioneer might help discover actual circumstances. If you have a serious interest in a reserved lot that does not sell, you might be able to negotiate a private sale by working with the auction house soon after the sale. Sometimes you find out that something didn't sell during the sale, perhaps when you've received the published post-sale price key. It may not be too late to inquire.

A Note on Reserves. It has long seemed logical to many that catalogs should include the amount at which an item is reserved. The caption would then specifically state both the reserve of $2,500, as in the illustration above,

and its estimated sale price of $3,000 to $5,000. No auction does this, yet. This practice would make it absolutely clear to potential buyers the minimum price for which the item can be purchased. This is definitely a quicksand area today. At some auctions one is not sure if any or all of the lots are reserved; if the reserve is above, below, or at the low estimate; and, when the gavel falls, if an item was sold or bought in.

How to Read Captions. It is recommended that you read descriptions in each catalog completely and very carefully, then reread them.

What does a caption contain, and what information is absolutely necessary? The necessary components in a decoy caption are the identification of the species, maker, the region where the decoy was made or used and the date it was made (if known). A description helps when pictures can't tell all. Is the decoy hollow or solid? Is it weighted (if so, is the weight original)? Is the neck nailed, screwed or pegged to the body? (and other salient features.) Present condition is *extremely* important. What body parts and paint are original? What are their current state? Has there been damage? If so, of what sort and to what extent? Are there repairs or restorations? Were they done poorly or expertly? Is the restorer known?

Lastly, some auction houses include an estimate at which price they believe the decoy will sell. It is generally listed between parenthesis, for example ($300–500). If the public is very, very lucky, the caption will indicate if a decoy is reserved and, if practices change after this book is published, the actual reserve dollar amount.

Additional information offered often includes where this bird (or one very similar to it) can be seen in books, magazines or show catalogs so readers can learn more about it or its maker. For example, the caption may read: "This exact decoy is pictured in color on page

119 of *Decoy Carvers if Illinois*, Parmalee and Loomis.'' Simply knowing it has been published builds novice buyer confidence.

Knowing who previously owned the bird allows the potential buyer to possibly contact them for dialogue, or just help document its more recent whereabouts: "From the Mackey Collection" (a most famous collector now deceased) or "This decoy was made in the 1930s for Merle Brown, Secretary-Treasurer of the Princeton Club from 1935 until 1950. The decoy was sold to Ted Vance around 1955 when Brown sold Vance his share in the club."

The caption may also be filled with subjective evaluations which may or may not be held by all observers: "*Exceedingly rare* bluebill drake in early autumn molt plummage by Elmer Crowell. This *outstanding* decoy is *extremely* full-bodied with a slightly turned head and *finely* detailed carved crossed wings. The paint quality is *exceptional*." This bird may or may not be all the writer says it is.

The careful reader must ask himself what the relevant information is within each caption. Beware of advertising hype and phrases commonly used, such as: "This is, without question, one of the finest. . .ever to be offered at auction." "Ex Collection of. . ." "Attributed to. . ." *Rare, very rare*, or *extremely rare*.

Specialty decoy auction houses, of which there are just a handful, may be congratulated for being among the few in any field of art and antiques who, on the whole, describe certain attributes of a lot, its condition, relevant information, and provenances to an extensive degree. We congratulate them!

So, learn to examine each caption with a critical mind. Lengthy captions may or may not provide helpful information regarding the actual condition, age, provenance, and rarity of an item. Following are a variety of captions chosen from different auction catalogs to illustrate varying descriptive techniques. Following each caption in parentheses is the name of the auction house, the date of the sale, and the lot number.

The first caption is full of information. This is the manner in which readers should expect catalogers to detail decoys and all other items. It's just what you want!

Rare hollow carved black duck circa 1910, by J. R. Wells, (Toronto, Ont.). "J. R. W. MAKER" brand in underside. F. N. on underside for Fred Nation. Nation was a founding member of the Oak Lake Shooting Club, established in 1907, near Brandon, Manitoba. Very fine paint detail and form. Condition: original paint with very minor wear; hit by shot, mostly on one side. The decoys that Wells made for the Oak Lake Club are considered to be his finest work. $5000–7000. (Julia, 4/1990, #569)

Condition descriptions which suggest intimate cataloger examination and a respect for absentee bidders (of which there are many) should be expected. The following captions for two Ward Brothers' pintails demonstrate a thorough examination by the cataloger.

Condition: Original paint with excellent patina and minor wear; several small paint rubs, mostly on head; tiny chip on bill tack and top of the tip of the tail; minor age line in underside; hairline crack part way through neck. (Julia, 10/1990, #553K)

For a Ward Pintail humpback you might see:

Condition: Excellent original paint with very minor wear; the end of the tail was broken off, but reattached by Lem Ward. He signed the underside of the repair "L. T. Ward Decoy Repair." At a later date the owner had the break redone more securely, and professionally touched up. Three hairline cracks in breast. (Julia, 10/1990, #121)

These are straightforward descriptions about decoys in quite acceptable condition.

Good, honest descriptions assist auctioneers in selling such birds at the strong price levels they have attained. Most collectors prefer to own decoys in good original condition, if possible; but most old working decoys are in less than pristine condition after decades of use under the gun.

Get to Know the Lingo. Since consignors and auctioneers need to attract potential buyers at all value levels, decoys are sometimes presented in the most flattering manner. This requires a broad range of alluring adjectives and creative descriptions. The need to describe thousands of decoys per year has also put a literary burden on auction house catalogers. To avoid being overly repetitious and more engaging, a new vocabulary continues to evolve. Verbage such as *professional paint strengthening, appears to have, old in use repaint, traces of original paint, inpainting, freshening,* and *taken down* have been introduced, each with a connotation to be deciphered by the reader.

Old or *recent in use repaint* means the duck was repainted. Professional or amateur *paint strengthening, inpainting,* and *freshening* mean the decoy has been, in an older vernacular, spiffed up. It has been repainted to some extent, usually by someone other than the maker. *Taken down* is a euphemism for stripping off one or more layers of non-original paint surface. Sellers would have you believe that *traces of original paint* is a positive factor; it probably means that very little of the first or original paint surface remains. But, that's all okay as long as you understand what it means. Read carefully. Once you're familiar with the lingo, keep your eye out for new phrasing.

Here are a few more to question. *Early.* Early in reference to what or whom? Early Ward Brothers decoys were made in the second quarter of the twentieth century, early Gus Wilson might be fifty years prior to an early Ward Brothers' decoy. *Mint* or *unused*

condition. Sometimes these two terms are used to describe birds made yesterday. *Essentially mint.* Well, is it or isn't it mint? *Good old paint, appears to be all original.* How would a catalog guarantee apply to those words? Same with *believed to be original.* Maybe it is and maybe it isn't, but that equates into a higher or lower dollar value. *Old in use repaint worn to original paint and bare wood in many places.* Interesting. *End of tail (or bill) has been chewed by a puppy.* You can buy it for less, get it professionally restored for a little, and be ahead pricewise—if you like the bird and don't own a puppy yourself! *Composition body.* That could mean papier-mâché, combinations of materials, or perhaps plastic foam—not the more desirable wood.

Watch out for the swans! It has been roughly estimated that well over half of all swans at auctions are new carvings—some out and out fakes. Often their captions are vague: "Canvas-covered swan, unknown maker. Condition: Old paint shows average wear." (Catalogs have been known to be in error about whether or not paint is really old.) Or: "Hollow carved swan from New Jersey. Branded 'Chip' on the bottom of tail. Condition: Excellent and original." Or: "Large swan with excellent form. Condition: Mint." When you study each of these actual catalog captions, you realize that what is said could be understood several ways and very little information is given.

A much better description of a real swan decoy reads: "Very early swan decoy in good honest old paint which is weathered, worn and chipped in many places. Originally found in a Maryland barn belonging to the Cockey family of Stevensville, Maryland, and possibly made by Jim Cockey. This decoy also has the form of decoys typically found in North Carolina and may have originated there." (Harmon, 7/23/90, Lot 126). No unsubstantiated attributions are made and the bird seems honestly described.

A sharp cataloger handles newer decoys

this way: "Large hollow swan, carved in the New Jersey coast tradition. Inset rectangular weight. 'Seabrook' is stamped in the underside. Made to look old. Condition: Original paint with minor wear; several scratches on back and sides; lightly hit by shot." (Guyette, 9/15–16/88, Lot 177M). Right away one understands that this is *not an old decoy!* That doesn't mean that the swan has no appeal. So be astute, read carefully, and learn to decipher auction catalog captions.

In order to encourage their clients to consider many of the lots offered, most auction firms also offer their expert opinions on the lots to be sold. Sometimes statements are based upon fact, sometimes upon personal preferences, and sometimes they are added in the hope of raising bidding enthusiasm. In most cases they are based upon the catalogers' long term experiences. *A rare decoy* is definitely a phrase overused to the point that it rarely carries much meaning; but it can occasionally be the truth. Rarity should be defined. Why is it rare? *One of the most important made by this carver* is, in reality, simply an opinion unless the statement is supported by fact. *So and so said it was the best shorebird he had ever seen.* Often, this is simply personal opinion. *Excellent, exceptional, exquisite, outstanding, superb* and other superlatives are plainly personal convictions which may or may not be of value to readers. In any poorly formulated caption, readers are forced to read between the lines. What was said? What wasn't said, and why?

Some descriptions capture a sense of history which might appeal to an individual's desire to collect a documented article. But, one must determine the reliability and extent of the documentation. For example:

Very rare robin snipe by Nathan Cobb Jr. (Cobb's Island, VA). This exact decoy is pictured on page 206 of *Southern Decoys* (Fleckenstein). This decoy was given by Arthur Cobb to Sarah Taylor (Oyster, VA), in the year 1901 to be used as a mobile hanging over her son William T. Taylor's crib. A small chain is stapled to the back to serve this purpose. Also included is Arthur Cobb's life saving instruction booklet, with his name written inside the cover. Both items have been consigned by descendents of Sarah Taylor. Condition: Original paint with minor wear; decoy has been heavily hit by shot; minor hairline cracks; several tiny chips. $2500–3500. (Julia, 4/1990, #82A)

This caption refers us to the book by Henry Fleckenstein. It also mentions that this shorebird was used as a crib mobile at the turn of the century. However, neither Fleckenstein nor the auction house accepting the consignment by the descendents of Sarah Taylor indicate written confirmation of this interesting family history. If it is an oral history, it should be stated as such.

When three first quarter nineteenth-century decoys sold in 1988, they evoked considerable discussion among collectors. They were a sleeping black duck, an old squaw drake, and a labrador duck attributed to Jacob H. Zabriskie (the initials JHZ and the year 1807 were stamped into the bottom of each). The catalog paraphrased family information this way:

Note: Jacob Zabriskie was born in 1772, and was a carpenter by trade in Paramus, New Jersey. This decoy and the next two have descended down through the Zabriskie family since they were carved by Jacob Zabriskie. All are extremely early decoys that possess a classic primitiveness, and to me [auction house decoy expert] represent some of the finest folk art to exist in the decoy world. A copy of the family background will go along with each one of these decoys. (Bourne, 6/1988, Lot #602–604)

It may very well be that J. Zabriskie did make these hunting decoys, but it is also possible that he did not. Perhaps he simply put his initials in the bottom to identify his rig. Per-

Attributed Jacob Zabriskie decoys.

haps someone else put the initials and date on the bottom. The catalog does not give additional family information which would help substantiate that this man was a known decoy carver/duck hunter or that other decoys by him are known to exist or were referred to in family documents. Were decoy making tools also handed down? A more definite attribution would require additional supportive data.

A similar situation involves the more well-known Long Island "Williams mergansers." Few decoys from the first few years of the 1800s have survived the nearly 200 years to the present. It would be even more exceptional to verify a lure back into the 1700s. However, since the 1960s, several natural roothead decoys have been credited to either a Roger Williams or T. Williams who, it is reported, lived on Long Island in the 1790s. Subsequently, one or more of these decoys have appeared in well-known public and private decoy collections, various museum exhibitions, folk art publications, and auction catalogs, usually with an indication of Williams (made 1790–1800) as the carver. In 1986, the

Smithsonian National Museum of American Art acquired a portion of the renowned Herbert Hemphill American folk art collection, which included a "Williams" merganser. The Smithsonian described it in the 1990 exhibition catalog in this manner:

> Unidentified artist, Merganser Duck Decoy, nineteenth century. . . Although this merganser drake has previously been attributed to Roger Williams of Sheepshead Bay, Long Island, no definite attribution can be assigned.

What this tells us is that attributions may eventually lead to more information on the decoy's background; but, they are, at best, just attributions. Good documentation is important. It also suggests that credible museums have more rigid standards than the majority of collectors, dealers and auction houses when it comes to documentation.

Historical evidence permitting definitive identification and provenance by the most dedicated historians does occasionally accompany decoys. It is important that factual records accompany a decoy whenever it changes hands. Here are some examples of decoys purchased from auctions *with accompanying provenance*:

An exceptional pair of Widgeon by Lloyd Sterling, Crisfield, MD. From an original rig of six (five drakes and only one hen), ordered from Sterling by Mr. George Charnick, at the time a high school junior, in 1925. They were purchased directly from Mr. Charnick in 1978 by the consignor who also tape recorded Mr. Charnick's recollections of gunning in Crisfield, stories of the Ward Brothers, and some interesting firsthand accounts on Lloyd Sterling and the way he made decoys. (Oliver, 7/1990, #363C)

An interested person should negotiate before the sale to receive a copy of this tape if successfully bidding on this bird.

Important pair of mergansers by Harald Thengs (Babylon, NY). This racey pair of decoys is one of six [actually five] pair of mergansers made by Thengs in the 1930s. . . He was a Norwegian immigrant who, after living in Babylon, New York, on Long Island, returned to Norway with all of his belongings, including a total of forty-six decoys. . . This historically important group of decoys was recently repatriated by Linda and Gene Kangas. See "Viking Decoys," Kangas & Kondon, in the spring issue of *Decoy Magazine*. (Julia, 4/1990, #696–698)

The published history of Thengs and his decoys was written with the assistance of a Thengs family member who provided a handwritten family history, documents, and memorabilia. A buyer could probably arrange to receive a copy of the *Decoy Magazine* article, and possibly a Xerox copy of relevant family papers.

A life-sized American eagle that sold at auction in 1987 included this original letter from the maker which was to go to the buyer: "To Whom it may concern: This is to certify that this is the one and only eagle that the Ward Bros. ever made. It was started in 1967 and completed in 1968. Signed L. T. Ward & Bro. Steve Ward/Lem" (Bourne, 3/87, #391).

A 200 word caption on a Caines Brothers mallard that sold in 1988 listed five books and magazines and one museum exhibition in which this particular decoy has appeared since November 1978. This type of information is an important part of its provenance, and while it does not definitively prove the carver or time period, the abundance of material and expert concurrence helps to confirm the authorship. The caption further states that "This decoy was a part of a rig of about eighteen birds shown in a motion picture entitled *The Day of the Duck Hunter* produced in 1916 by Paramount Pictures. Some still photos from this motion picture were included in an article which appeared in the November 1917 issue of *Field & Stream* magazine (pages 600 and 601)." (Oliver, 2/88, #55).

Personal research on the part of a prospective buyer would find these facts to be accurate. This dates these decoys to at least the early 1900s. In addition, an article in the well-known publication *North American Decoys* on the history of the Caines Brothers of South Carolina and the decoys they made for the renowned Bernard Baruch of Hobcaw Baronny, Georgetown, identifies the decoys to the makers.

An early Black Duck by A. E. Crowell with good original paint, replaced head, carved and painted on Crowell's style. Condition: Overall good. (Oliver, 7/91, #227)

See if you can decipher what this is actually saying and what was probably intended.

No one should expect perfect auction catalogs, articles or books. There are often typos. Only meticulous, time-consuming proofreading can rid a text of all these insidious errors. Usually time constraints do not permit this. Photographs are sometimes transposed on a page and end up with each other's description. Obviously, this is not intentional. Very often errors exist because little information is known or reluctantly passed on to the auction house or catalog writer by an owner.

Back in the 1970s, travelers to the Caribbean discovered numbers of actual working turtle net floats made and used by native fishermen to decoy or attract live turtles to their nets. These life-sized wooden turtle shapes were attached to catch nets and helped to keep them afloat. Some of the turtle decoys were brought into the States; unfortunately, a number of them temporarily lost their identity as they moved into the collecting culture. In 1976 one of these equatorial turtles was included in an exhibition at The Brooklyn Museum, New York, and the Los Angeles County Museum of Art titled "Folk Sculpture USA." This may have been its debut in a professional situation and, regrettably, it was incorrectly captioned as:

> Reportedly from South Carolina, this is one of two known examples of turtle decoys (there are many more than two). It was probably made early in the 20th century. Painted wood, length 29″. Collection of Michael and Julie Hall.

A distinctive looking sea gull resided in a well-known mid-western folk art collection for many years. In 1974 it was publically exhibited and also included in a popular folk sculpture book. In the show at the Cranbrook Academy of Art in Michigan, it was noted as "artist unknown, early 20th century, Maine." In *American Folk Sculpture* by Robert Bishop, the gull was still listed as a Maine bird but was then dated circa 1940. By 1983 Dale and Gary Guyette, researchers of the decoys of Maritime Canada, had published definitive identification of this sea gull. On page 161 of their singular work *Decoys of Maritime Canada* is a photograph of "Amateur Savoie in his barbershop/workshop, holding a sea gull that he carved in 1961, signed, dated, and temperature recorded (90° F). Photo circa 1982." This gull is a replica of the previously published decoy, and now the Savoie gulls stand correctly documented. It is the constant search for information, and its publication, which helps set records right even after years of inaccuracy.

Collectors should be aware that decoy auction catalogs are some of the most complete and buyer-helpful on the continent. However, if a firm does not guarantee their descriptions, how helpful are they? Progressive auction houses who expanded into the decoy market in the 1970s and 1980s made the acquaintance of hundreds of savvy, informed collectors and dealers with years of experience in that hitherto mostly grassroots field. Results were immediate. Buyers were quick to demand extensive catalog descriptions which were to the point and accurate, as well as guarantees by the house.

CHAPTER SEVEN

How to Buy at Auctions

Be Prepared

Prior to previewing, study your catalog at home. Preview times usually are set just before the auction begins, but you might be able to make special arrangements for an earlier showing by contacting the firm. Once you've established a relationship with them, they might answer specific questions over the phone as well as providing you with photographs other than those in the catalog, X-rays, and videos.

If you have a good catalog, why should you preview? There are many reasons. First and perhaps most important, things often look different in person. Photography can enhance or fail to illustrate particular features. When previewing you can pick up and feel the object. In your hands, subtleties may become apparent. These could be difficult or impossible to notice in a catalog. Size is also hard to determine from an illustration. How large or how

small something is might influence your appreciation of it. A personal response to such intangibles probably would be a strong influencing factor on each person's level of interest. For example, a very worn, well-used decoy may appeal to some while a crisp, mint, unused artifact may not.

If you cannot attend the preview in person, there are still several options to consider. You might persuade a friend traveling to the auction to preview for you and call you with a detailed report. You can also hire a professional to do the same. Their charges range up to ten percent of the gavel price. The auction house will also be willing to offer a more detailed description over the phone. Remember, firsthand previewing is best because it may offer you perspectives different from those derived from the catalog or the telephone.

Bidding

It is before an auction begins that one should decide how much to bid. At this point you are

calm and rational about all aspects of the purchase, which include quality, condition, and your personal need to have the decoy. However, many people leave the decision making process to when the item is on the block and get caught up in the heat of the moment, often paying more than something is worth, or more than they feel comfortable spending. The smart way to buy at auction is to determine how much you will pay and write that figure in the catalog beside the lot number. Then stick to your decision!

Hold Up Your Hand!

After registering in person to bid, you will be assigned a bidding number. This number is usually preprinted on a card or paddle which you show the auctioneer when you are bidding and when you are successful so his people can record that you bought a lot. You may also bid by written absentee, by telephone during the auction, or by using a representative.

A wide assortment of bidding techniques and strategies occur during auctions. Some inveterate buyers feel that if no one knows they are buying, it is to their advantage. They are very circumspect when motioning to the auctioneer. Instead of simply holding their paddle or hand in the air to signal, a very cautious buyer may surreptitiously nod his head, touch his glasses, change position, flick his catalog. . .whatever he makes up and indicates to the auctioneer ahead of time.

Many stand at the very back of the room, hopefully behind everyone else so they can see who is bidding against them and not be too obvious to others. We've seen one man stand around a corner and appear only when signaling to the auctioneer! Another used a pay phone to call an auction employee in the same room to have the employee do his bidding for him. That way, no one was supposed to know he was interested in that lot. Most of the time, the audience as a whole is not totally aware when carefully planned practices are in play. For example, there might be several different people bidding up to set levels for the same person so that his interests are not apparent as a pattern during the bidding. An individual might be present at an auction and yet write his bid in absentee fashion. These practices help him to maintain anonymity or capitalize on an air of phone bidder mystery.

If you are unable to attend the auction, you may possibly preview at an earlier date and leave a written bid, call in a bid based upon your research which the house will record, use a representative or friend who will be attending the auction to bid for you, or arrange to be on the telephone during the bidding of the particular items you want and participate as if you were there. These are all common practices.

We once conceived of a successful strategy after observing an ongoing bidding technique that appeared to intimidate other bidders. A particular bidder was almost always successful in winning lots for himself or for a friend. Their interests were often directed toward high profile items with high values. This bidder simply raised his paddle up and kept it there until successful. Over time, others soon learned that it was almost fruitless to compete. Cognizant of this, we asked this individual, who was a friend, to bid on a rare decoy for us using his technique. Because he was bidding on our behalf, we were not going to bid, although one of us would be present during the auction. As the bidding started, he raised his paddle for us and held it high; the faces of other interested parties immediately expressed discouragement. How could they compete? Thanks to his most appreciated help, we were able to acquire what we very much wanted and at a price considerably lower than we expected to pay.

These are basic bidding procedures which work well in most cases. Novice auction goers should sit where they can see and be seen by the auctioneer. You definitely want to be seen when you bid. As hard as the auctioneer works to acknowledge everyone and bring them in as active participants, many bidders often go unnoticed.

The Opening Bid

The auctioneer will usually try to encourage the audience to begin with a substantial dollar figure on an expensive bird. For instance, he may ask for an opening bid of $3,000 for a decoy he expects to bring $6,000. When no one responds, he'll drop to $1,000. Someone will raise a hand and the auctioneer accepts the bid. On a lot such as this people will usually be asked to bid in increments of $1,000, $500 or possibly $250 so the lot will sell quickly and well. On an item expected to bring $500, the opening bid may start at $100 or below and proceed in increments of $100, $50, or even $25; often the audience determines the figure. Be aware of the bidding increment.

Another bidding technique is to let several people begin the bidding, raising the amount to a figure where most stop trying to buy the item, then raise your hand for your first bid. This might suggest to others that you have just begun. Those remaining may think to themselves, ''What's the use, this person's real serious'' and quit. At the very least, you have not helped jump the price up by adding fire to the first flurry of bidding.

Keep your eye on the auctioneer so you will know when he is indicating to you, asking if you want to continue. If you do, then bid. If you are not going to bid any higher, shake your head no. Keep your price limits in your thoughts constantly. Stay firm! Now, it is certainly possible to jump into the action again just by raising your hand; but the most important thing for someone new to auctions is to set a limit on what they want to spend, then quit cold when that limit is reached. There is definitely such a thing as auction fever. Many people get it. They are undisciplined. They may have great control in other aspects of their lives, but at an auction when the bidding is ripe, they just can't resist going a little higher and a little higher. It's like the gambler who figures the next throw of the dice will land his way or his next hand of cards will win the pot.

You might also consider exerting a little control in a bidding situation by hesitating each time the auctioneer points in your direction before indicating a yes bid. This helps slow the pace down and may possibly keep the winning bid lower. However, if you want to appear bold and determined to win the item, be very quick to respond or simply keep your hand or paddle in the air until the bidding stops and you are the buyer.

Procedures vary at each house after you win a lot. At some, a runner or house employee brings a voucher to your seat for you to sign immediately, acknowledging in writing your purchase and the price. The runner may or may not bring the item bought, depending again on house methods. At other auctions, you needn't sign anything and you can pick up your purchases after paying for them. Of course, you may pay and leave the auction at any time.

Premiums to the Buyer

In addition to the obvious gavel price, many auctions charge a ten percent buyer's premium. In other words, the buyer is charged extra for doing business with them. It means that if you buy a decoy for $300, there is an additional charge of $30. Therefore, the purchase will cost you $330. A bid of $1,000 will actually cost $1,100, and a $10,000 dollar bid would incur an additional $1,000 charge! Remember to calculate this amount into your bidding limit. If buying in person, sales tax might be another charge to consider. Purchases made from or shipped to an out-of-state address often do not require payment of sales tax, but packing and shipping charges should be anticipated.

Premiums to the Seller

Auction houses traditionally charge each *seller* a percentage of the gavel price. This percentage is usually based upon the quality of the merchandise, so percentages will vary. When you hear or read "10 and 10," it supposedly indicates that the buyer and seller are both being charged the same percentage. However, that is not actually the norm. Many *sellers* are often charged more. "Ten and whatever the traffic will bear" is probably more accurate. Therefore, when buying or selling, make sure you are fully aware of the circumstances.

If you are interested in consigning decoys or related sporting artifacts to an auction, shop around; don't base your decision only on percentages. Begin by sending good photographs with detailed descriptions to firms for their consideration. Discuss your options with each of them and find out how they value your items, how and when they would sell them, and what percentage they would charge you. For example, timeliness might be a consideration important to you. How soon would your birds be auctioned, and how quickly will the house pay you? Find out if other costs might be billed to you such as photography, advertising, shipping, buy-in fees and insurance.

A person with an unusually expensive decoy expected to bring over $10,000 dollars might negotiate a lower consignor premium with the house. On the other hand, someone with low grade/low collector interest decoys might have to pay 15 to 20 percent. Therefore, the better the consignment, the less the seller might pay. Auctioneers know that it is more cost-effective for them to sell fewer birds val-

ued under $500. It might take them a minute to sell a $200 decoy and another minute for a $2,000 bird. They would earn a $20 buyer's premium on the first, and $200 on the second. It is no wonder that fewer and fewer low-priced decoys are offered at major auction houses today.

The quality and type of items to be sold should also be considered when choosing an auction house. Selection is important. Less valuable pieces might actually sell quicker and for more money at small, local auctions. There, the audiences are generally less informed and perhaps have regional interests (incentives). It might also be prudent to consign a small group of items as opposed to selling only one at a time. The reason is simple. Specific auction results are unpredictable, and by selling a group you will hopefully attain an average price because some things sell better than expected and others not as well.

People sell to make money. They also sell to thin out their collection, add other items to their collection, change directions, or to reinvest the funds in some other manner. Remember that the selling prices of standard or common items often reflect the condition of the economy at the time of the sale. Trends may also influence price levels. Rare collectibles, however, are not the norm and their level of success at any time is almost impossible to accurately predict.

Services

Most auction houses are eager to have your business, either as a consignor or a buyer. To that end and because they usually enjoy their business, they are most helpful. *For the seller*, they give free appraisals and often help determine if the timing is right to sell certain items. For major consignments they have been known to arrange a pick up at your house. *For*

the buyer, they will provide larger or better photographs and X-rays, and answer your questions in person or on the telephone. In their catalogs they provide information on airline transportation to their city; directions to the auction house; and lists of local hotels with addresses, phone numbers, and prices. Many houses arrange discounted hotel rates for auction goers. So it can be with pleasure and anticipation that you pick and choose the houses you will work with and buy from. After all, *they* should be trying to please *you*.

Estimates

Many auction houses provide prospective bidders with a printed educated guess at what amount they believe their consignments will sell. They take into account previous sales of similar items, condition, the economy, and many other factors. These estimates are either printed in their catalogs at the end of each lot description or may be obtained by talking privately with the auctioneers. For example, $200–300 at the end of a caption indicates an educated opinion that the selling price should be somewhere within this range. Since firms sell many things over a period of time, they soon develop a perspective to base estimates upon. For different reasons, some estimate high and some low; so decide for yourself what the value is to you.

All specialty decoy auctions usually include a mixture of both old working decoys and newer waterfowl carvings. A variety of related sporting art and artifacts are also blended into the sales. Auctions provide a tremendous educational opportunity to study firsthand the many different decoys and to make new contacts, ask questions, learn values and trends, solicit opinions, develop your library, and hopefully add to your collection.

CHAPTER EIGHT

Fakes and Alterations

No price range is immune to the fake decoy. Bogus decoys of various qualities exist at all levels. Some folks are happy to earn just a few dollars for their reproductions, other counterfeiters think bigger. This means you might pay $50 or $50,000 for a fake decoy. . .unless you are careful.

Legitimate Impersonators

Traditionally, artisans have made replicas of historic decoys because those particular forms interested or pleased them. Some contemporary names you might become familiar with are Frank Finney, William Gibian, Tom Langdon, Mark McNair and Lou Schifferl. Each has developed his own personal style as well as a following of collectors for his work. Usually, their designs are purely personal interpretations of waterfowl; but, on occasion, some have made exact copies of popular gunning decoys by earlier known and unknown makers. In the fine art world, these contemporary craftsmen would be "copyists" when reproducing existing decoys. For the most part, they sign their carvings. Frank has used a nicely lettered "Finney" on the bottoms. Most use their initials, as Mark did on his earlier birds (MSM). Later he changed to

Virginia-type robin snipe, by contemporary artist Mark McNair, made to look old.

"McNair." Each one signs most, but probably not every, duck carving made. Without a signature, a novice with an untrained eye could easily be fooled.

However, while there is no intention by these artists to have their birds recognized as old working decoys or to deceive unsuspecting collectors, all too often it happens. Unless everyone in the world is familiar with the particulars of an artist's style and output, then not everyone is going to recognize an artist's waterfowl carving. In the general marketplace some of these birds become, at least for a time to some people, a decoy. This is confusing and sometimes costly, as illustrated by the following experience.

A distinguished New York City folk art collector purchased a beautiful old-looking swan decoy from a New York City folk art gallery for thousands of dollars. He proudly admired its gracefulness, and displayed it prominently within his personal folk sculpture collection alongside a few notable decoys. Shortly after he acquired it, a knowledgeable decoy collector visited his apartment and recognized the swan as being a noted contemporary artist's work. Disappointed because he thought the bird an old decoy and because it had been represented to him as old and rare, the collector returned the swan to the gallery for a refund. Armed with newly gained information regarding the carver of the swan, the collector recovered his purchase price. The old-looking bird, unfortunately, was unsigned and the artist who made it did not orginally sell it as old. That happened later. Did it happen again? Possibly.

What Is a Fake?

An outright fake decoy is a bird carving which is intentionally made to create and maintain a false impression. The fake is an imitator of a duck carving, which itself is imitating a live duck. So we have an imitator imitating an imitator!

However, it is important to understand what is, and what is not, a larcenous deed. A waterfowl carving (a duck, goose, or shorebird) can be manufactured and/or altered for any number of innocent reasons. Many amateur and professional craftsmen enjoy carving these enchanting aquatic creatures. Some present day hunters continue to make decoys for their personal rigs. Hunters of the distant and not-so-distant past refurbished their decoy tools whenever necessary. Collectors and dealers, in order to preserve a decaying artifact, have overseen restoration of many historic decoys. One can expect to find examples of all of the above every day in this collecting field, and they may all be honest decoys.

Nevertheless, there is every need to be aware of the *intent* at the time of the creation or restoration as well as the *intent* when the decoy is sold, traded, or given away. When a decoy is passed along and known fakes or alterations are concealed, we have a situation which could be fraudulent.

There are numerous scenarios to consider. Following are some examples.

A gentlemen in his seventies made his own hunting rig of wooden decoys forty years ago. He is too old to hunt any more and sells them all to a friend. This first step from the boathouse is all on the up and up. The friend, a flea market dealer, decides the decoys don't quite look old enough, so he doctors them up in time-honored ways, triples the price he paid the hunter, and sells them off. The dealer has deliberately tried to make the birds *appear to be something other than what they are*. He has converted an honest group of working decoys, which were probably sold one at a time. What did he tell prospective customers? What was written on the bill of sale? After all, he knew the name and location of the maker, when they were made, and how many were made. More than likely, none of that historic information went with each sale.

A picker finds a shack full of older, paint-worn decoys. However, he discovers, after doing some homework, that they were made by a well-known deceased carver. He knows that had he been lucky enough to find them in good condition, he would stand to make a lot more money when selling them. His dilemma is a common one and he chooses a course often taken. The decoys are carefully repainted (totally or partially) to closely resemble, possibly duplicate, the paint of the original maker, then sold without explanation. Not good!

A couple of decoys—bodies only—have been kicking around for a decade. Finally, it is decided to find some heads and fix them up. Sometimes any old head will do if the body is nondescript. Other times, a well-known body deserves to be married up with a head by the same carver or factory. This may take more time to assemble, but the practice is rather commonplace. Now, there is nothing essentially wrong with either of these practices! In fact, either one makes good sense. Using the decoy as a tool, a frugal person makes repairs rather than discarding it. All the oldtime hunters were thrifty and commonly reheaded decoys when necessary. The problem comes in the collecting stage. When a known reheaded decoy is sold without that information being passed along to the buyer, then the seller is negligent. The question of intent must be addressed.

The same is true in countless other situations. If a buyer discovers alterations in a decoy after he has purchased it, or has restorations made and then sells it omitting what he knows, history remains clouded and the buyer is deceived. So, a fake decoy is one which has intentionally been passed along under false circumstances.

Unseen damage often affects an entire collecting theater when new collectors innocently purchase forgeries. Here are excited, innocent individuals who should be guided carefully by the experts so that they learn how to collect, who to see, where to go, what books to read, which museums to visit, what is untouched and what is restored, and what might be fake. All too often, however, these charming and enthusiastic novices are shamelessly taken advantage of both by ignorant peripheral dealers and the knowledgeably greedy. New collectors often become disgusted when they eventually learn that they have wasted their enthusiasm and hard-earned money on fakes. They might assume that they will never be able to tell the difference, and distrust everyone associated with the field. Most are irretrievably lost as potential friends and colleagues. This has happened time and again. Some collecting areas have nearly been devastated by widespread avarice. For a quick buck, the unscrupulous cause the loss of innumerable eager people who might one day have contributed greatly to the collecting field.

The general perception of a fake is one that has been totally fabricated from scratch to simulate an authentic decoy. A fake decoy is created to make someone money. Oftentimes *many people* make money from subsequent sales of a fake decoy. Often these are copies of decoys made by well-known, extensively publicized, and massively collected deceased carvers. These cost unsuspecting collectors a lot of money because they are eager to buy famous works by such celebrated carvers as John Blair, Elmer Crowell, Albert Laing, Joseph Lincoln, and the Ward Brothers. Fakery often follows a great carver's works, some more than others. The great numbers of Ward Brothers decoys which were not made by either Lem or Steve Ward is frightening. And that is fakery of just one sort.

Changes to an original decoy can also constitute fakery. Ideally, all changes, repairs, or restorations to a decoy should be obvious to the viewer and/or documented on paper. Most are not! Because decoys bring more money if they are in good, original condition, many restorations are undertaken to make the bird ap-

Authentic early Dudley canvasback in back with artist/restorer Frank Finney's rendition in front.

pear as if it had never been injured. As a buyer, you should educate yourself and/or find a confidante to help you make ticklish judgments concerning condition. Don't hesitate to get second and third opinions.

One midwest collector usually waits until after he has made a purchase to ask questions. That is not a productive method. Another person never asks any questions. He appears to think that if anyone else knows he is interested in a certain item, they will buy it out from under him. His paranoic method is to keep his own counsel totally. A certain measure of this may be wise, however, one either doesn't learn anything at all that way or learning is slow and expensive.

So, technically, a fake could be a bona fide old decoy which has been restored in some manner, with subsequent buyers being totally unaware of the restoration. There are a number of things to look for when considering an attractive purchase. The paint could be partially or totally new. Chips or chunks from different body parts such as the bill, head, neck, and tail could have been replaced. The bill could have been broken and partially or totally replaced. One or both eyes could be new or the neck putty restored. Sometimes you find a new head on an old body or new body with old head. You can even find a new head on a new body!

Now, it is just fine to buy a decoy which has repairs or restorations. Many do! After all, they were tools of a trade and often suffered hard use or abuse. Better to save the artifact than to discard it or allow it to fall into total disrepair. One just has to remember to relate the price paid to the overall condition of the decoy. An artifact in all original condition will command a higher price than the same which has been restored. Another consideration is rarity. Very rare and very old decoys in need of restoration should probably be properly restored. Their existence and value will thus be maintained.

Who Makes the Fakes and Secret Repairs?

The forger earns money from an endeavor that basically costs only the price of a block of wood and some paint; the rest is often a labor of love, and/or greed. Forgers are often talented persons who truly enjoy their own artistic endeavors. The sad part is that their choice is limited to copying others rather than creating personalized images and establishing their own names.

The Creator

Each generation finds the preferences of its people slightly different from the last. Food, transportation, furniture, clothing, and art are all continually modified and altered as the years go by. For the most part, each generation loves and is comfortable with its own time period. Therein lies one of the secrets of forgers. While they tend to create artifacts based on an earlier generation's traditions, the new creations are intended to appeal to the more recently developed aesthetics. This usually has little to do with whether or not a decoy, for example, was a successful hunting implement. The faker must imbue a ''working decoy'' carving with charismatic and artful styling which is appealing to contemporary tastes. This type of decoy will prompt an unsuspecting collector to shout, ''Fabulous!''

How does the fooler do it? In the same manner that art forgers have been working for centuries—they work to please the buyer. If you remember this, you will find yourself beginning to question decoys which are *too* attractive. Remember, there is nothing wrong with asking questions.

The most creative and artistic fakers design ducks to seduce your senses. Their birds grab your attention because they know what you want to see! Some may choose more exotic species like racy mergansers, graceful swans, cocky sea gulls, and handsome, bold eiders—ducks with a little mystery! Each is carved and painted with grace, style, and pizazz, and given a one-of-a-kind look. Some have twisted necks; others have fattened bodies; and others are hollowed to be extremely lightweight. Then it is made to look old. The unsuspecting collector says to himself, ''Goodness, look at that gorgeous decoy. I've got to have it!''

The Restorer

This is a talented artisan, often making a living working for collectors, museums and auction houses. They may mend, rebuild, repaint, and sometimes rework pieces. It has been the unfortunate custom for collectors and auction houses to request that items be made to look as they did when new. Therefore, all repairs are concealed expertly. Reputable museums generally want the repair to be known. If accurate records do not follow an expertly restored item to each subsequent owner, this information is soon lost and the artifact becomes ''near mint,'' ''all original'', or ''a great example.'' Before and after restoration, photographs should be taken and made a part of this record. Ask for them. Talk to restorers.

The Fix-It-and-Sell-It Guy

It is much easier to see repairs that have been made quickly and with less finesse than those made by a professional restorer. In fact, the non-professional repairs are almost preferrable because you are less likely to be fooled by them.

The Seller

Many collectors become adept at repairing, inpainting, and fixing up. Just because something has been in a collection for a long time doesn't insure that it hasn't been re-paired. The seller may have honestly forgotten work done two decades earlier. Good record keeping will help retain more accurate information.

How Do They Do It?

A Whole New Bird By Hand

The conventional way to make any duck, goose, or shorebird decoy is to carve the body out of one block of wood, fashion the head and neck from another piece, then glue and nail the two together. Most working decoys and their impersonators are made this way. They are usually hand-carved from start to finish using a hatchet or band saw for the basic body form and various knives and chisels for the shaping. Sanding finishes the surface. Therefore, basic construction characteristics between the real and the replica are similar.

Often, parts of the same decoy are from different sources. A number of years ago, we were looking to acquire a ruddy duck because we didn't have one in our collection at the time. Since ruddys congregate in just a few areas of North America authentic ruddy duck decoys are rather scarce and difficult to find. However, one Memorial Day weekend at a public gathering of decoy people, a southeastern dealer brought a charming little ruddy which tickled our acquisitive fancy. It was obviously hand-carved; the neck was attached to the body by square nails. We studied its style, carefully looked at the bird's weathered and aged-looking surface, and talked about the price of $800 and whether or not the bird was genuine. We also asked a few other collectors, dealers, and one well-known auctioneer for advice. They all gave a thumbs up. Well, we bought it; but also asked for and received a bill of sale describing the decoy as a genuine working ruddy.

Eventually, a niggling of doubt about the bird developed in our minds on the long ride home; and it wasn't long after arriving that we began to thoroughly examine the ruddy again. The body styling was in keeping with other ruddys we had admired, indications on the bottom of the bird suggested rigging had been attached, and the outside surfaces still looked right. We decided to telephone a trusted friend and southeastern expert. We told him about the ruddy and our growing suspicions. He confirmed that a small rig of old ruddies had recently been found but only one body had a head and he knew where that decoy was. Now, the impulse to remove the head from the body and examine an inside surface was too great to ignore. The moment the neck was separated from the body, a great wave of the scent of a cedar forest wafted around our heads. That was instantly a dead giveaway that the wood was fresh! A fifty to one hundred-year-old decoy does not smell like a cedar closet. The aroma should have long since dissipated. The exposed nails weren't oxidized and some of the glue was still wet. We had an honest, one-hundred- year-old body with a brand new head.

One significant act had been to obtain the bill of sale which included the stipulation that the bird was an old decoy. We quickly stopped payment on our check, packed the body and head separately in the same box, and shipped them back to the dealer. We later found that the same dealer had made similar transactions with other collectors.

Remember, we had asked people before our purchase of the ruddy, and they had given us their opinion that the bird was genuine. Always keep an open and inquiring mind about your purchases. Keep probing for information. Often you'll get tidbits which over time add to the decoy's provenance sheet and your histori-

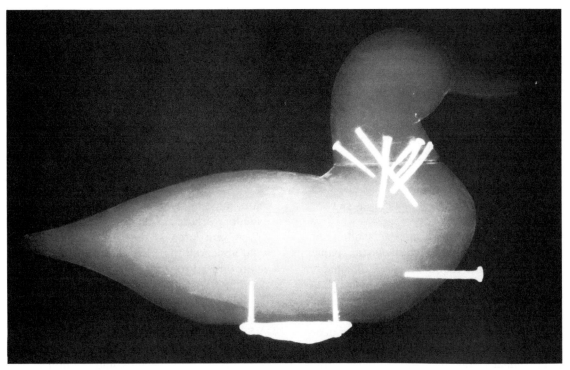

An X-ray of a *reproduction* John Williams ruddy duck. A convincing fake on the outside, the inside reveals no rusting nails, shot marks, stressed wood, repairs or other signs of age and hard use in salt water expected of an old decoy.

cal knowledge of the bird. Sometimes, there are revelations of another kind. Both are to be sought. Both are equally important.

Of equal significance is knowing the reputation of the seller, whether he is a collector, dealer, or from an auction house. During our inquiries, we kept asking about the man who had the ruddy for sale. Some people you ask may be friends or business partners and you won't get an unbiased answer to your inquiry. As you widen your interviews, you will eventually gain a more impartial perspective, as we did. You learn never to stop admiring *and* analyzing.

Machine-Made Decoys

The first lathe-turned decoys in Maryland came off a newly developed duplicating machine in 1924. Until that time, most individuals roughed out decoys by hand; but those who began using this new process saved a great deal of time. Factories such as Mason and Dodge utilized duplicating equipment as early as the late nineteenth century. Obviously, counterfeiters of today can capitalize on the same equipment. The lathe process uses one finished or original decoy as a master form for the basic cutting process of new blocks of wood. One, four, six or more blocks are automatically cut out at a time—faithfully replicating the original on the machine.

Here's an example of how two nefarious fellows utilized this method to underhandedly copy one well-known collectible decoy. This took place in the 1970s. A collector was ostensibly considering the purchase of a friend's decoy. He asked to take it home for a few days in order to make a decision. For a friend, permission was, of course, granted, and off went the decoy. Later, for one reason or another, the decoy was returned. Unbeknownst to the owner, the "friend" and a buddy had put the bird on a duplicating lathe and made several replicas which they then painted and probably sold as the real thing. The deed was discovered by an observant collector who, when later admiring the original decoy, noticed evidence of unnatural holes hidden in the bottom of the decoy. Upon reflection, it was decided that the bird had to have been attached to a duplicating machine, as no other means explained the particular pattern of the new marks. The owner of the bird then remembered the only time the bird had been away from him. Some friend!

How to Tell a Fake From the Real Thing

Examine Decoys Closely

Decoys made from materials other than wood such as fabric, metal, plastic, papier-mâché, cork, and rubber are also collected but by fewer people. Consequently, most fakes are made of wood or of materials made to resemble wood.

While previewing a recent summer decoy auction on the east coast, we noticed a bird quite similar to one we had owned for a number of years. It was described in the catalog as "A rare sleeping canvasback drake by Ben Schmidt, Detroit, MI. Mint condition in all respects," and estimated to sell for $400 to $600. Interested, we picked up the bird and handed it to one another. As the catalog said, the canvasback was in very fine condition and quite attractive; but curiously, it felt too heavy. True, there was a small weight fixed to the bottom, but not the characteristic wood and leaded keel Ben always attached to his working decoys. So, the heaviness wasn't in the uncharacteristic attachments. It was the body itself which was heavy, too heavy for the cedar Ben used for his birds. Upon closer scrutiny of the bottom, we found that the wood seemed to be denser than cedar. Our thoughts were that it was most likely a high-pressure polyurethane casting taken from an original Ben Schmidt sleeper, and painted in his style. We had heard rumors about the existence of these, but had never seen one. This item sold for $1,127.50, quite a bit over the high esti-

mate, most likely because it appeared to be in excellent original condition.

A year later, at the same auction house, what appeared to be the very same decoy was again offered for sale. The catalog cited, "A sleeping canvasback drake by Ben Schmidt, Detroit, MI. Excellent original condition in all respects." The estimate this time was for $300 to $500 and it sold for $715. This brings up a few obvious questions. If the decoy sold last year for $1,127.50, why would the house estimate be lower this year? Was this a rigmate to the previous decoy? Or, was it the same one? If it was the same decoy, one scenario could be that the first purchaser also thought or discovered that the decoy wasn't an original wooden Ben Schmidt. It was either returned to the auction gallery, or simply submitted for auction a year later. This might indicate the reason for a lower estimate. If the decoy was a fine, wooden Ben Schmidt, the second auction estimate should most certainly have been at least in the range of $1000. In fact, we sold our own authentic Schmidt turned head canvasback sleeper in a private transaction several years before for $1200. That would then seem to be the appropriate price range.

Casting polyurethane under pressure into a strong aluminum mold to make facsimile decoys was known to have taken place a decade ago. An expert painter then reproduces the original carver's paint style, and suddenly there are more decoys on the market. Such reproductions can pass along easily into the

Old Canada goose heads. Very often, found body parts are married to other old or newly made parts.

decoy collecting system and through numerous hands before they are detected.

Actually, one should expect to find some refurbishing in every decoy, then set about trying to detect *all* of it. Some have none. Try to prove to yourself what is right and what isn't. With this attitude of discovery, you can learn a great deal by examining hundreds of decoys over time. But don't think you are expected to gain all of this knowledge by yourself. One of the great rewards of collecting is the give-and-take of the friendships that develop based upon a shared hobby. You will learn through many interesting people, and you will help them, too.

What Does a Fake Look Like?

Usually, it looks pretty good. However, you can only decide what a fake is after you

have learned what real decoys with real age look like.

The most obvious way to recognize fake decoys is through surface clues. In most cases, an indepth examination of exterior characteristics should tell the story. The paint and wood of an old working decoy will show varying evidence of the changes it has naturally undergone: dryness, cracking, crazing, flaking, chipping, layering, color changes from oxidation, and dirt and grime in the crevices may all be apparent. Loosened neck joints and bill scrapes or damage might appear, and rigging or remnants of rigging may remain. If you learn all you can about how real decoys should look after years of use and misuse, dirt, storage, and general aging from the elements (sun, atmospheric conditions), then you can become more confident in evaluating them.

Patina

A decoy which has been exposed to the elements will have a natural, slowly aged surface color (patina). The whites will appear in any number of shades of "old lace" and the color tones will usually have softened and mellowed or turned much darker than when new. The paint tones should be consistent with one another; the white on the chest should have the same tonal quality as the white on a speculum or a cheek patch. If they do not, this indicates there has been some repainting at one time. After looking at hundreds of older decoys aged by the elements, it becomes possible to spot inconsistencies. Look for them. Inconsistencies are not necessarily fakes; they are clues to the real story.

Recently repainted decoys are often subjected to various chemicals and techniques to change the bright look of new paint. One of the easiest and more common quick methods is the application of an oil or polish containing a stain. These are available in all hardware stores (*Baer* brand, *Old English*, etc.). We are always glad when a faker uses this type of solution because it is immediately identifiable on white paint. From twenty feet away, the decoy looks like somebody *Old English*ed it, which means the bird probably has been recently repainted (partially or totally).

Decoys redone by more learned painters will not be so readily apparent. They won't use a tinted furniture polish for effect. They have spent many hours becoming good painters, experimenting with chemicals and heat and other techniques used for effect. They have done their homework and are aware of the intricacies of paint changes.

Canada goose exhibiting actual signs of a naturally-aged decoy: Dry wood and paint, raised wood grain and separation, worn and crazed paint down to bare wood in places, rusting nails, and shot marks.

This honest, old eider has many layers of working repaint and normal body checking due to repeated yearly exposure to the harsh northeastern elements.

Crazing

The painted surfaces of many older decoys show crazing (cracks) in some areas. This is because the wood and paint expand and contract many times but at different rates. The end result is a breaking up of the smooth paint. Mostly, there will be several rather small crazed areas on different parts of the bird. Some restorers simulate this effect with a chemical process. Crazing solutions can be bought over the counter. Some work well and some work too quickly. The crazing of a naturally aged surface will show differences in size, thickness, and texture; it won't be consistent. Chemically induced crazing often appears uniform and over a larger than normal area. So,

part of your education should include the minute examination of many decoy surfaces with a magnifier. Learn what old paint looks like.

Wear

Surface rubs can indicate actual or simulated patterns of wear. A well-handled decoy will exhibit areas where the surface has been rubbed. Normal areas of wear are the lower sides, the tip of the bill and tail, and carved wing tips. But these are usually a well-mottled, softly eroded area. Someone trying to fake wear will usually rub the new paint off the high spots of a duck: the top of the head, chest front, and shoulders. This looks purposefully hand rubbed and is easy to spot.

This early Louisiana teal may have been exposed to high temperatures when stored which could account for the typical bubbled, crazed and flaked paint. Some individuals try to imitate such signs, but it is difficult to duplicate the effects of long-term aging.

Body Marks

A solid, oversized black duck made by Ralph Coykendahl and used on Merrymeeting Bay, has small shot holes scarring the right side of the its body and head. In fact, one shot is still imbedded in the right cheek below and behind the eye. Along the bottom edge of the left side of the bill a sliver of wood is missing; the telltale half-round shapes left by shot just above it. This bird, as do most, tells a story. It describes a rather harrowing time on the water when, if possible, the decoy may have wondered if the hunter was trying to kill him or his live counterpart. It indicates that the live duck was on or very near the water when the hunter fired, hitting his decoy in the process of killing his supper. A little more sportsmanship might have been in order that day.

This visual story allows the collector to conclude that the decoy is authentic. The shot scars make it easy for even a beginner to see that this Coykendahl decoy is in original paint. Where the paint is rubbed totally off, the bare wood has aged to a soft brown. While holding decoys like this and moving them around in your hands—feeling the head and bill and stroking the sides—all you feel is a roundness. There are no sharp edges. The decoy has achieved its maturity.

A new, faked, or redone decoy often tries to emulate some of these characteristics, but usually fails. And, that's good for us collectors! Shot fired into the body during a faking process are usually embedded straight on whereas on the moving water during a hunt, the shots would normally graze or hit the decoy in odd places. If a decoy is hollow and you can hear shot rattling around inside but cannot find where it entered, chances are the decoy has been repainted.

Reworked decoys sometimes mimic the surface abuse lures often suffer while on the job. Nicks, chips, rubs, and dings are commonplace. Sometimes they are hardly noticeable and sometimes they are all over the bird. But when such marks appear to have been caused by a large group of keys, chains, and other distressing tools, it is apparent that you are viewing manufactured stress. Beware. These are not the tool marks of a one-of-a-kind production.

The underside of a decoy that has been rigged and used has sustained certain physical changes relevant to the addition of keels, weights, line ties, corrosion of screws and nails, and surface erosion caused by the water (sometimes salt water). If such things are not evident, then the decoy may be old and unused; used, repainted and not used since; or just plain newly made.

By studying decoys from particular hunting regions, or from all regions, you will become familiar with the typical rigging used in each. Certain carvers are known also by how they outfitted the decoys for use. You can do some of this at home with your library of reference books. You will come to know the look of old nail holes after a keel or weight has been removed, the rusty evidence of a line tie eyescrew long subjected to salt water, and the oxidation of bare wood on the bottom. Soon, you will be able to tell from the belly of a decoy if it has been redone or is new.

Where Will You Find Fakes?

Most anywhere. Actually, the majority of fresh "old duck decoys" exist in the under $150 price range. One does not have to be an artist or even a gifted carver to make a lower priced duck or goose, and there are many places to sell them. You can find these bogus birds at garage sales, large and small flea markets, antiques shops, gift shops, mall shows, and local auctions.

More accomplished hands will make fakes which can be sold for several hundred or thousand dollars. The most masterful of these can beguile even some experienced collectors and dealers. Fake decoys of this level could turn up at national auctions, as well as museum and private collections.

Museums that get decoys sometimes receive them as donations or bequests, and some often accept outright what they are given. Sometimes it may be just one or two birds, other times a whole collection. Because they do not all have an expert curator or consultant to help them evaluate before acceptance, they may acquire some inappropriate carvings along with the good ones. The Shelburne Museum in Shelburne, Vermont, has a top-notch collection based primarily upon the decoys of five early collectors. The Shelburne decoys are housed in a separate facility on the museum grounds and have been actively curated for many years. It is well worth visiting.

At one time in the late 1970s, a small group of decoy experts was invited to Shelburne to evaluate all the museum's decoys. Previously unknown carvings were properly identified by region and maker, duplications were recognized, conditions were assessed, and some decoys were discovered to have been reheaded and/or repainted during their years as working lures. It was during this process that the curator found that there were no fake decoys in the collection. Anything that wasn't in original condition had simply been honestly refurbished during its working years. Shelburn's records were then updated to reflect the new information.

Some museums have an ongoing evaluation of their decoys, either through their own

These Fritz Geiger decoys show an overall wear on their painted surfaces because they were handled, bumped, scraped and scratched through many seasons of duck hunting. Artificially distressed surfaces usually show more uniformity.

curators, who keep up with new publications in the field, or through guest and volunteer experts. However, some other public exhibitions are maintained by unknowledgeable curators and might welcome expert input.

Private collections, on the other hand, usually receive constant attention and appraisal as the collector adds to, evaluates, and occasionally subtracts from the grouping. Even then, a not-so-right bird may fly in the door. A not uncommon occurrence was related by an experienced and astute observer who was a longtime student of decoys. For quite a few years, he owned a decoy which he had carefully chosen and purchased. The admired and appreciated bird filled a certain place within a grouping of important shorebirds. Eventually, the time came when he considered selling it, and a prospective buyer took the bird outside into bright sunlight to see it better. Only then, did the expertly replaced head become apparent!

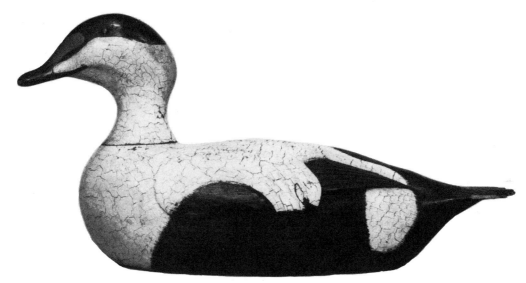

This eider drake was attributed to Charles Hart in an auction. Inconsistencies such as heavily and evenly crazed white paint, smooth clean black paint, broken wing tips, heavy wood weight and no indication of ballast system raised several questions.

How to Avoid Fakes and Misrepresentations

Auctions

People often equate buying at auction with fast decisions, bidding fever, and making mistakes. On the contrary, buying from an auction which provides a good presale catalog and guarantee is one of the safest ways to acquire an authentic decoy. (See Chapter Six, Understanding Auctions.) Here's how you do it.

Order the catalog four to six weeks before the auction date; it will probably arrive one to two weeks before the sale. At home, you should have plenty of time to relax and look at every picture, read many of the captions, and make a list of all lots that interest you. Study each decoy that interests you and those that don't. You might discover items that are totally new to you.

Use a powerful magnifying glass to scrutinize each photograph. Compare what the caption tells you with what you can actually see. Check each condition report against the photo. Can you see the crack in the neck, the paint worn down to bare wood on the right side, the shot mark on the side of the head? Good. Now, look at the photo for things the caption may not tell you. Does the shade of white paint on the chest seem to be different from that on the speculum? Is there a glass eye where the maker nearly always used tack? Is the bill the right shape? The bird appears to have a side seam but the caption didn't mention it was hollow. What you are doing is evaluating each decoy that attracts your attention even before seeing it in person. Usually during this process, decisions are made as to whether or not you really want it and at what price level. Some you desire more, some may drop lower on your list. Some are eliminated.

The next step is to get out your decoy reference books and compare the photos of the birds you like at auction with similar documented examples. Look at body, head and bill styling as well as the way the maker painted each species. Are the ones in the auction the same? Jot down any questions your comparison raises. Re-evaluate your interest.

Here is where your decoy friends can help. Contact them and discuss the birds you are considering. Refer to the ideas that your study has brought up. Get several opinions about authenticity, condition, and price; maybe even a little about bidding strategy. They may even know who previously owned or consigned the bird.

And, lastly, go to the auction and see the birds yourself. Pick them up, turn them around, notice all the cataloged and uncataloged points. Compare two birds by the same maker, if possible. Look for similarities and differences. Ask someone you know is knowledgeable to look at some birds with you and comment on them. Often, they'll help you. Reciprocate in some way.

Birds at auction offer you the opportunity to do much pre- purchase study. Leisurely examine the catalog many times, use all reference materials, talk over the birds with friends, see the birds in person, ask for expert advice on the spot. When you put all these steps together, the chances of getting a bird you don't want are low. Examining items in person may also change the order of your priority list. Something that didn't look good in the catalog may really appeal to you in person. More importantly, you've learned a lot in a short time.

If you find a decoy at an uncataloged auction, which eliminates virtually all of the steps to confident buying discussed above, your chances of making a bad purchase increase. However, should a knowledgeable decoy person be in attendance, you could ask for on-the-spot advice which might lower the risk. Of course, that person may have a personal interest in the item, perhaps he consigned it or wants to purchase it. Find out.

Private Sales

Usually, a private sale affords the same opportunity for research as a good auction. You start by seeing the bird in a *good* photograph or in person, at which time the owner tells you about it. You can make quite a bit of headway from a good photo. Go through all the previously discussed strategies. If you conclude that the decoy seems to be what you want, then make arrangements to have the decoy sent to you on approval for a specified period of time. The seller often pays the shipping one way and the buyer pays the return charges, if necessary. Usually the buyer will send the seller a check. Upon receiving it, the seller sends the decoy with the guarantee that he will hold the check for so many days, until he hears from the buyer by telephone for a final decision. Be prepared to make that final decision quickly. If there is an expert in your area, make arrangements beforehand for him to see the bird in person as soon as you get it. There is no shame in turning down the bird at this point. It is just business. No hard feelings.

If you are buying privately and are away from home, the most important thing to remember is to take your time. You needn't conclude the deal immediately. Take some good photos home with you and proceed as already suggested. It may also be possible to take the bird on approval. Get a written, explicit guarantee!

Conventions

Things often move faster at a decoy show or convention. You might be concerned that if you don't commit to a bird immediately, someone else will walk up and buy it. That is a possibility, of course. But if you are seriously considering a decoy in this situation, sit down and have a long talk with the owner. Let him tell you how he got the bird and what, if anything, has been done to it over the years. Discuss price. Let him tell you about the maker. *Get to know the owner and the bird a bit.* Then, if you still want it, ask him to allow you first refusal (your chance to take it or leave it before anyone else) during the next hour. During that time you can ask others to look at the decoy and discuss its merits. Be thoughtful enough to let the seller know your decision right away, whatever it is.

The best thing going for you in this situation is the great number of experienced decoy collectors, dealers, and authors milling around, some of whom might be willing to help you out depending upon your reputation, approach, and relationship with them.

A motel convention is a more casual place than an auction. You can strike up conversations with almost anyone about decoys. Walk from room to room, booth to booth, and table to table and chat about decoys and prices. It's a great place to study decoys and make friends.

Flea Markets

Now, here's a dangerous situation! Usually no one admits to knowing anything about the decoys they have, and they don't seem to care to know. Rarely does one admit to owning a book on decoy identification and history. Generally, the quality level is rather low and prices are in the $50 to $150 range. Back in the 1950s, '60s, and '70s, one could regularly find a good decoy at flea markets. Today, it's less likely. This is not to say a great bird won't turn up. A few decoy dealers do set up at flea markets and they are knowledgeable and helpful.

Every experienced collector has a favorite flea market story. Once we were at a very small racetrack show in Medina, Ohio. There seemed to be nothing at all to catch our eyes until we spotted a familiar-looking bird on its side on a dealer's table. We picked the decoy up and began a conversation, asking the dealer where it was from, what he knew about it, and how much he wanted for it. The man confidently commented that it was "a shorebird from Wisconsin and the price was $125." It was hard to contain ourselves as we happily paid him the full price and left. Shorebirds from Wisconsin would be a rare commodity at best. But this, we knew, was a full-bodied standing sea gull made by famous lighthouse keeper/decoy maker Gus Wilson of Maine. Our surprise discovery made for an even more delightful morning. We collect Wilsons.

Remember, it's best to be cautious. If you find a nice looking decoy, but you're not sure if it's right, take some good photos, proceed cautiously, and research.

What to Do with a Fake

Most everyone buys a bogus decoy sometime. When you accept this as inevitable, the best attitude is to consider that the purchase price includes protection. You are entitled to a written bill of sale or guarantee which includes the name and signature of the seller, date of sale, price, description, condition, and date of decoy. Don't just let your check be your receipt. If the bird is not right, the existence of a complete, descriptive receipt usually motivates the seller to reimburse you without question. Should that not be the case, the receipt, along with expert testimony from an impartial decoy authority, will probably impel a court to settle in your favor.

Getting Rid of It

In the past, most people have gotten rid of their questionable decoys exactly the way they received them—with no information. They sold them privately or publicly by disguising or omitting the truth of some imperfection. In a transaction, if a buyer does not ask a specific question about authenticity or condition, he may not be told some very important information. This is an omission rather than a lie by the seller, but he is nevertheless culpable.

If you are unable to return the decoy to its source, you own it. When you decide to let it go, you may not be able to recover the purchase price. That's okay. Consider it "tuition." By experiencing firsthand a mistake, you will have analyzed the decoy, its problems, and the manner in which you made your purchase. This lesson is impressed indelibly in your mind, hopefully never to be repeated. Remember, people pay to go to college. Your tuition may actually save you a lot of money in the future. You might decide to keep the decoy as a reminder or as a study piece.

You can certainly always sell the decoy privately or at auction. An auction catalog allows you to publicly present the decoy as you know it. Do not be shy when praising the bird's merits or when listing exactly what has happened. Following are some examples of everyday auction catalog talk that presented some nice lures in a positive manner, even though they were not mint. Our comments are in brackets.

"Rare 1932 Model Black Duck by the Ward Brothers. See *Ward Brothers Decoys*, Gard and McGrath [for same or similar bird?]. Fine paint detail and patina [notice the praise]. Condition: Original paint with very minor wear; most of bill is a very well done professional replacement [by whom?]; professional restoration to a crack in the neck." [Heavy on 'professional'—helps to sell the bird.] (Julia/Guyette, 10/90)

This caption describes the bird in glowing terms even though it has had major surgery!

The following defines desirable birds with some shortcomings, which are quite acceptable. As a prospective buyer, always study entire captions.

"Fine Black Duck by Ira Hudson (Chincoteague, VA). Painted by the Ward Brothers [does not say "repainted"—read on]. Slightly turned head. Condition: Excellent repaint by the Ward Brothers [repainted, but not by the maker], minor wear on underside, minor age line on underside, hairline crack on back and breast." (Julia/Guyette, 10/90)

"Redhead drake Lowhead by Nate Quillen, circa 1890. In rare original paint which is in excellent condition. From the Barber rig. Old bill repair has been recently redone. Paint on bill is not original [how could it be?]." (Harmon, 7/90)

"Merganser hen [Cape Cod] with carved, raised wings. Condition: Head is an old replacement [who replaced it?] and has been repainted by K. E. DeLong [a professional restorer], body has been taken down to its original paint [by Delong] showing average wear. (Note: Found in a house in Sagamore Beach just across the bridge from the Cape.)" [So what!] (Bourne, 7/90)

"Fat Jaw Blue Bill drake by the Ward Brothers (Crisfield, MD). Condition: Appears to be reheaded [what does "appears to be" mean?]; old in-use repaint [how old?]; several age lines on underside [how many, how big, and are they problematic?]. (Julia/Guyette, 10/90)

It is no sin for a decoy to have been used so hard that it required new eyes, new paint, or even a new head! But if you have paid a lot for a decoy without knowing its true condition, you have made a mistake. So, keep your mistake or sell it listing *all* its shortcomings. You'll sleep well at night knowing you have become better educated and can move forward as a result.

CHAPTER NINE

Regional Photo Essays

The Northeast

The Northeast area of North America includes hunting regions located in Quebec, New Brunswick, Prince Edward Island, Nova Scotia, Maine, Vermont, New Hampshire, Massachusetts, Connecticut, and Rhode Island.

Quebec decoys are noted for their highly intricate surfaces that are distinctly different from any other region of North America. This is exemplified by the classic work of Orel LeBoeuf.

Carvers on *Prince Edward Island* (P.E.I.)

Rare red-throated loon from the northeastern region, possibly carved by a 19th-century North American native.

Bluebill drake by Henri Laviolette (Quebec).

Black duck by Bill Cooper (Quebec).

Goldeneye drake (front) and bluebill hen by Orel LeBoeuf (Quebec).

made more full-bodied stickups than those from any other area. Their stickup brant decoys in active poses are worthy of any collection. John Ramsey and Adaniga Marks are two prominent makers whose works are recognized as the best of P.E.I.

Nova Scotia decoys tend to have low, flattened profiles, occasional raised wings, and flat bottoms. There were several different schools of carving within the province.

Decoys from *Maine* tend to be large and bold for use on rough ocean waters. Many have inletted necks. Augustus Wilson is the state's best-known and most collected carver.

He is also considered one of the most creative makers from any region.

A wide variety of decoy types were produced in *Massachusetts*. Everything from sleek mergansers to mammoth slat geese represent the state's styles. There are many well-known makers.

Two major schools of carving existed in *Connecticut*. Decoys made along the Connecticut River and in and around the town of Stratford typify those styles made by Sam Collins, Sr., Benjamin Holmes, Albert Laing, and Charles Wheeler.

Eider hen by Oscar L. Crowell (Nova Scotia).

Goldeneye drake by Robert Paquette (Quebec).

Eider hen and drake from Grand Manan Island, New Brunswick, signed C. F. Jacobs.

Hollow sea gull by Mic Mac Indian (P.E.I.).

Brant by unknown maker (P.E.I.).

Brant by John Ramsey (P.E.I.).

Loon by the Levy family (Nova Scotia).

Merganser pair by Willie Ross (Maine).

Merganser with mussel in mouth by Leigh Witherspoon from Vinyl Haven (Maine).

Eider drake by Maurice Decker (Maine).

Goldeneye drake by Sam Webb, Sr. (Vermont).

Preening surf scoter by Gus Wilson (Maine).

Cork pintail drake by Elmer Crowell (Massachusetts).

Eider by unknown maker (Maine).

Two eider hens by Pete Mitchell (Maine).

Canvas-covered Canada goose by George Boyd (New Hampshire).

Canvas-covered old squaw drake by Lothrop Holmes (Massachusetts).

Canada goose by Joe Lincoln (Massachusetts).

Merganser hens by Captain Preston Wright (Massachusetts).

Black ducks by Charles Hart (Massachusetts).

Preening Canada goose by Elmer Crowell (Massachusetts).

Gadwall by Cassius Smith (Connecticut).

Pintail drake by Charles "Shang" Wheeler (Connecticut).

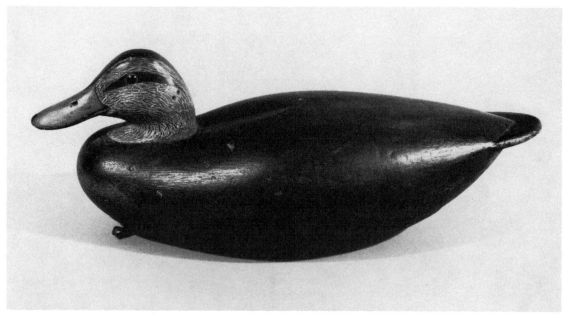

Black duck by Ben Holmes (Connecticut).

American merganser by Sam Collins, Sr. (Connecticut).

Sleeping bluebill by Albert Laing (Connecticut).

Old squaw drake by Art Baldwin (Connecticut).

The Mid-Atlantic

The Mid-Atlantic sector includes the hunting regions of New York State, Long Island, the Delaware River, and New Jersey.

Most of the decoys found in central *New York* were used either in the Thousand Island area or the Finger Lakes region. Most of the lures from New York were solid bodied. Frank Coombs, Chauncey Wheeler, Samuel Denny, James Stanley, Roy Conklin, and Julius and Robert Mittlelsteadt are some of the more publicized carvers.

The shores of *Long Island* have a rich waterfowling history. The earliest documented non-native decoys were made there, attributed to Roger Williams, circa 1790–1810. Other nineteenth-century carvers were Obediah Verity, William Bowman, and Thomas Gelston.

Along the banks of the *Delaware River* are found distinctive, hollow, round-bodied, low-necked river decoys. The two main carvers were John English and John Blair, Sr.

Most of *New Jersey's* decoy production occurred along the Atlantic Coast. New Jersey is famous for its hollow, two-piece symmetrical decoys. Probably the most prolific and most famous New Jersey maker was Harry V. Shourds of Tuckerton.

Bufflehead drake by J. Montrose Hungerford (New York).

Canvasback by Chauncey Wheeler (New York).

Redhead pair by Ed Barnhardt (New York).

Canada goose by Roy Conklin (New York).

Red-breasted merganser by unknown maker (Long Island).

Old squaw drake and hen by Harald Thengs (Long Island).

Cork black duck by unknown maker (Long Island).

Scoter by William Bowman (Long Island).

Bluebill drake by John Blair (Delaware River area).

110

Pintail hen by Bill Quinn (Delaware River area).

Wigeon drake carved by John English; paint attributed to John Dawson (Delaware River area).

Oversize, resting black duck by Jess Heisler (Delaware River area).

Canvasback pair attributed to Charles Allen (Delaware River area).

Brant by Birdsall Ridgeway (New Jersey).

Bluebill pair by H. V. Shourds (New Jersey).

Canada goose by Sam Soper (New Jersey).

Canada goose (field type) by James Mittlesteadt. (New York).

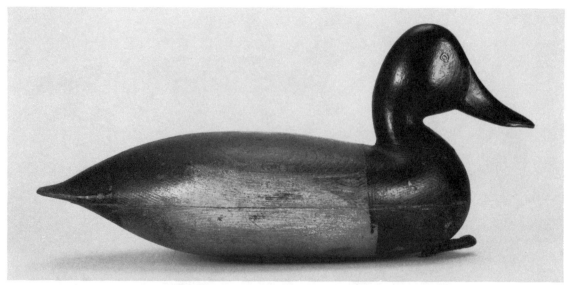

Bluebill by Rowley Horner (New Jersey).

Red-breasted merganser by George Harvey (New Jersey).

Back preening black duck by unknown maker (Long Island).

The Central Atlantic

The Central Atlantic region includes hunting areas in the *upper* and *lower Chesapeake Bay* as well as the shore lines of *Virginia*. There were probably more decoys made along the upper bay than anywhere else in the country. Three nineteenth-century carvers who hand-chopped their decoys were John "Daddy" Holly, William Heverin, and Benjamin Dye. The majority of the early twentieth-century decoys were solid-bodied, lathe-turned lures. Madison Mitchell and Robert McGaw's decoys were popular. Lower in the bay in the town of Crisfield, another style was popular-ized. Those decoys tended to be wide, flat-bottomed birds produced on a much more limited basis. The Ward and Sterling families are credited with developing the region's style.

On the eastern shore of Virginia and Chincoteague Island, however, the decoys were quite different. A number were hollow, some had inletted necks, and others raised wing tips. Famous carvers from these areas are Dave "Umbrella" Watson, Ira Hudson, Miles Hancock, Charles Birch, and the Cobb family.

Swimming Brant by Nathan Cobb (Virginia).

Bluebill pair by Arthur H. Cobb (Virginia).

Wigeon by Lloyd Tyler (Maryland).

Goldeneye drake by the Ward Brothers (Maryland).

Pintail drake by James Holly (Maryland).

Canvasback by James Currier (Maryland).

Wigeon by Madison Mitchell (Maryland).

Canvasback drake by L. Travis Ward, Sr. (Maryland).

Canvasback hen attributed to Will Sterling (Maryland).

Hooded merganser drake by Doug Jester (Virginia).

Canada goose by Walter Brady (Virginia).

Pintail drake by Ira Hudson (Virginia).

Swan by Charles Birch (Virginia).

The South

In the southeastern area of the United States there was a tremendous amount of waterfowl hunting, but decoys are only found in numbers from North and South Carolina and Louisiana.

In *North Carolina*, solid-bodied lures were used to hunt black ducks, Canada geese, canvasbacks, mallards, ruddy ducks, and swans most often in large rigs numbering in the hundreds of decoys. The Dudley Brothers, Alvirah Wright, John Williams, and Mitchell Fulcher are North Carolina carvers whose works are sought after today by collectors.

And, in *South Carolina*, the Caines Brothers are the only makers of merit.

In the bayou country of *Louisiana*, each local parish evolved its own characteristics. However, many Louisiana decoys tend to be made with a French flavor from lightweight woods such as tupelo and spanish cedar. There are many documented Louisiana carvers including Mitchel LaFrance, Charles Joefrau, George Frederick, and Nicole Vidacovich as well as the Vizier and Whipple families.

Ruddy duck by Ned Burgess (North Carolina).

Canvasback by the Dudley Brothers (North Carolina).

Ruddy duck by Alvirah Wright (North Carolina).

Swan by unknown maker, Swan Island Club (North Carolina).

Caines black duck (South Carolina).

Ruddy duck by John Williams (North Carolina).

Three swimming mallard hen "mini chasers" by Mark Whipple (Louisiana).

Mallard drake and hen by the Caines Brothers (South Carolina).

Canada goose by the O'Neil family (North Carolina).

Mallard drake by Charles Armstrong (Louisiana).

Pintail hen by Charles Joefrau (Louisiana).

Pintail drake by Nicole Vidacovich (Louisiana).

Mallard drake by Alcide Cormardelle (Louisiana).

Preening mallard drake by Mitchel LaFrance (Louisiana).

Pintail drake by Mark Whipple (Louisiana).

The Midwest

The extensive Midwest region of the continent includes Canadian hunting areas in the provinces of Manitoba and Ontario as well as the states of Illinois, Indiana, Michigan, Minnesota, Nebraska, Ohio, and Wisconsin. Because of the great size of this classification, a tremendous diversity of styles exist.

There are five or more definable styles in *Ontario*. They range from hollow, smooth-bodied decoys to highly textured, solid-bodied lures. Carvers such as Thomas Chambers, George Warin, the Nichol family, and Samuel Hutchings illustrate this variety.

Decoys from *Illinois* are referred to as Illinois River. At least 75 percent of those were made as two-piece hollow constructions. Their rounded bottoms are typical of river decoys. Charles Perdew, Robert Ellison, and Bert Graves carved in this manner. However, Fred Allen, who carved in the nineteenth century, made wide, low, flat-bottomed lures. In *Michigan* there are generally lightweight, hollow decoys made in the nineteenth century; but the twentieth century saw considerably different ones designed as larger, solid-bodied blocks. Representing these two time periods are Nate Quillen and Ben Schmidt.

The northwest corner of *Ohio* was where most decoys have been made and used. Private hunt clubs in the nineteenth century accounted for the best of the area. Ned John Hauser of Sandusky is one of the earliest documented carvers from any area on the continent.

In *Wisconsin*, there are several different area styles. The two most prominent are from Lake Winnebago and Milwaukee. The Milwaukee School is characterized by realistic-looking waterfowl portraits.

Canvasback hen by the Ducharme family (Manitoba).

American merganser hen and drake by D. W. Nichol (Ontario).

Teal by John Wells (Ontario).

Early Canada goose by George Warin (Ontario).

Redhead hen by Ivar Fernlund (Ontario).

130

Hollow bluebill hen by D. K. Nichol (Ontario).

Blue and green-wing teal drakes by William Ellis (Ontario).

Mallard hen and drake by Bernard Ohnmacht (Indiana).

Mallard hen by Edward Keller (Illinois).

Bluebill grouping by Paul Lipke (Indiana).

Canvasback in original paint by Catherine Elliston (Illinois).

Mallard hen and drake by Charles Perdew (Illinois).

High-neck mallard hen and drake by Walter Dawson
(Illinois).

Canada goose by Charles Schoenheider, Sr. (Illinois).

Standing mallard drake by "Frank Pl—z—" (Illinois).

Mallard drake by Charles Walker and mallard hen by
Judge Glen Cameron (Illinois).

Standing mallard drake by John Tax (Minnesota).

Folky canvasback by Harry H. Ackerman (Michigan).

Rare pre-Civil War bufflehead by Nate Quillen (Michigan).

Pintail hen by Miles Pirnie (Michigan).

Canada goose by Ben Schmidt (Michigan).

Bufflehead drake by Tom Schroeder (Michigan).

Goldeneye drake by John Schweikart (Michigan).

Mammoth canvasback drake by John Zachman (Michigan).

Hollow canvasback by Ned John Hauser (Ohio).

Hollow black duck used by J. H. Porter at Winous Point (Ohio).

Blue-wing teal used by R. White at the Ottawa Club (Ohio).

Cork Canada goose by William Enright (Ohio).

Ringbill pair by Owen Gromme (Wisconsin).

Bluebill drake by Joseph Seiger (Wisconsin).

Pintail drake by Walter Peltzer (Wisconsin).

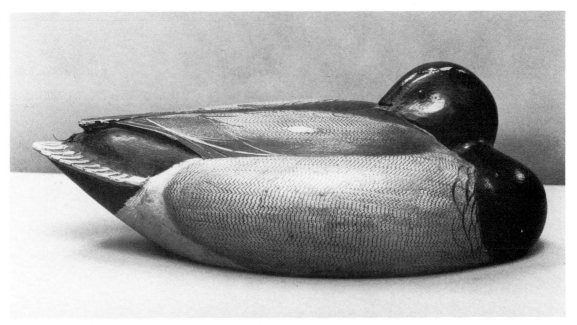

Sleeping mallard drake by Ferd Homme (Wisconsin).

Mallard hen by Clair Markham (Wisconsin).

Two styles of canvasback drakes by Gus Moak (Wisconsin).

The West

The Pacific coastline of North America stretches from hunting areas in California up through Oregon, Washington and into British Columbia. Due to the distances involved, styles vary considerably. Large, hollow, simple birds are found in *British Columbia* while smaller, solid-bodied carvings are more typical of southern *California*. Popular among collectors are works by Percy Bicknell, Charles Bergman, William McClellan, Horace Crandall and Richard Janson, to name just a few.

Pintail drake by unknown maker (British Columbia).

Pintail and mallard by Percy Bicknell (British Columbia).

Mallard hen by Charles Bergman (Oregon).

Brant by unknown maker (British Columbia).

Preening cork pintail by unknown maker (California).

Pintail drake by John Patterson (California).

Pintail hen and drake by Richard Ludwig Janson (California).

Cinnamon teal pair by Luigi Andrucetti (California).

Balsa shoveller hen by John Tornberg (California).

The Shorebirds

Shorebirds include a lengthy list of species of birds most commonly found along the eastern seaboard during their annual migrations. They spend their time feeding on land instead of on the water where most ducks are found. Shorebirds are often found running along the shorelines in search of small morsels of sustenance, and it is from this vantage that the waterfowler hunted these tiny birds for food and feathers. Small carved replicas were mounted on rods and jammed into the wet sand near the waterline, enticing the birds to feed within his gunning range.

It was the excessive hunting of these little birds which brought about their near demise and the extinction of at least one species, the Eskimo curlew. Federal laws banned all shorebird shooting by 1920. Therefore working shorebird decoys date before that decade. Species commonly hunted during the nineteenth century included names familiar to bird watchers as well as present day collectors of shorebird decoys. Some of them are the black-bellied and golden plovers; long-billed, Hudsonian and Eskimo curlews; greater and lesser yellowlegs; marbled and Hudsonian godwits; dowitcher; knot; sandpipers; and ruddy turnstone.

Shorebird decoys are one of the best areas of collecting in the field for several reasons. Compared to the larger ducks and huge geese, they are the little gems. They are small, delicate, and do not take up much room in the home. They are some of the oldest decoys as a group since the legitimate ones were made before the twentieth century. There are many species with a wide variety of color in many active feeding and moving positions. There are enough shorebird decoys still in existence for many people to collect and enjoy them separately and together. They are, at present and as a whole, the most reasonably priced collectible decoys (most shorebird decoys can be purchased for between $200 and $1,000). There is enough beauty and history in shorebird decoys to fulfill the desires of many.

Eskimo curlew by Clarence Gardner and Newton Dexter, Little Compton, Rhode Island.

Two curlews by Harry V. Shourds, Tuckerton, New Jersey.

Feeding golden plover by Elmer Crowell, East Harwich, Massachusetts.

Black-bellied plover by Obediah Verity, Long Island, New York.

151

Cork peeps by Hewlett, Long Island, New York.

Curlew by Nathan Cobb, Cobb Island, Virginia.

Black-bellied plover by William Bowman, Long Island, New York.

Dowitcher by John Dilley, Quogue, Long Island, New York.

153

Golden plover and feeding black-bellied plover by Elisha Burr, Hingham, Massachusetts.

The Factory Decoys

Decoys made on a production basis are not classified by regional dictates because they were designed and sold to hunters throughout North America. By way of explanation, let us first look at non-factory decoys.

The identification of non-factory decoys begins first and foremost with recognizing the styling and carpentry common to each waterfowling region. Each area's hunting conditions, most especially the body of water on which the decoys were placed as lures, dictates criteria for successful hunting tools including guns, boats, blinds and decoys. Meeting these criteria in each area in the nineteenth century were a fairly homogeneous group of people solving the problems and usually mimicking the successful adaptations of their neighbors. In the 1800s there were over twenty major regional waterfowling hunting areas from which a particular styling of hunting decoy evolved. Within each locality tens or even hundreds of individuals made decoys for themselves as well as for their friends or the local townspeople who weren't handy with a knife.

A hunter/carver in the market hunting days often found his decoys in great demand by others, which kept him busy for many months of the year. It occurred to some that this could be a profitable full-time profession. Decoy factories often developed out of these one-man operations with just the carver himself or several employees doing assembly line work. Some operations included the use of a duplicating lathe which turned out rough bodies and heads which were then hand finished and painted. As their reputations spread, some advertised, sold, and shipped their decoys throughout the continent by rail. Because they were servicing hunters in various regions, they often styled the decoys to be adaptable to a variety of regional requirements. Some factories advertised that they would make anything a customer required.

These factories sprung up in the last third of the nineteenth century and some are still in

Oversize premier grade mallard hen and drake by the Mason Decoy Factory, Detroit, Michigan.

Red-breasted merganser drake by the J. N. Dodge Decoy Company, Detroit, Michigan.

operation today. Each factory's output had its own recognizable characteristics of body and paint design as well as manufacturing techniques not necessarily in line with the regional characteristics inherent in decoys of the vicinity in which they did business. Therefore, factory decoys are most often studied and portrayed apart from regionally identified decoys.

Pintail drake and mallard hen by Lifelike Lures, New Orleans, Louisiana.

Wigeon drake by the Harvey A. Stevens Decoys Company, Weedsport, New York.

Teal and wigeon pairs by Wildfowler Decoys.

157

Two-sided cast metal owl decoy with moveable wings by Soules and Swisher, Decatur, Illinois.

Set of six stuffed decoys with real feathers in original box by Decoys Delux, Morrison, Illinois.

CHAPTER TEN

Maintaining, Cataloging, and Protecting Your Collection

Maintenance

Working decoys exist in every conceivable state of disrepair, and that is how it should be. There are decoys which have been hunted over for decades and stored for years in hunting sheds surrounded by damp, oftentimes salt-laden air. Some have been lovingly cared for between seasonal duties and others have never seen a day on the water or a duck overhead. Most, however, do exhibit the wear and tear of an exciting outdoor life. Collectors should expect to encounter lures with no heads or no bodies, with all original paint or none of it, with shot holes, broken tails, dog-chewed bills, and mismatched eyes. There may be dry

This wonderful George Warin Canada goose needed a professional bill restoration to complete its profile when offered at auction.

rot, sun- melted paint, and missing hardware; chinks and rubs, cracks and body checks, and knotholes; and previous repairs. Any decoy can exhibit these conditions to a greater or lesser extent.

To repair or not? To restore or not? If so, how much? Collectors constantly ponder these questions as they acquire decoys. There is no rule of thumb, no established standard, and until now, no definitive answers. How does each collector decide what to do? Up until the present, they have made their choices based upon their own abilities, but usually without knowing the accepted *best* ways to care for decoys.

Care and Cleaning

The least injurious way to clean a painted wooden surface is to gently wipe or blot a dirty decoy with a damp cloth, being careful to identify and avoid any flaking paint. From that time on, dust with a soft, lint-free cloth only when necessary. It is common to see crazed, dry, peeling paint on old decoys. If it is original paint which is chipping, the bird should probably be taken to a paint specialist. It is possible to have paint flakes reattached; and in cases of valuable artifacts, this should definitely be done. Trained museum conservators and restorers of fine art are located across the continent and can be easily contacted. Get to know one in your region.

Upon acquiring a new decoy "in the field," many collectors simply wipe off dried mud and old water stains before storing or displaying. Others polish or wax the surfaces because they like the way an applied finish seemingly emphasizes paint color, and some think varnish protects the original painted surface from flaking. More than a few pull off weights, pads, keels, and rigging. Others leave them on as evidence of the decoy's profession. It's important to realize that a few of these practices are harmless, but some are destructive!

Oils. Did anyone ever tell you that you need to feed the wood? According to conservators at the Shelburne Museum, Winterthur Museum, The Cleveland Museum of Art and the New York State Historical Association, there is no such thing as feeding the wood in the art of artifact preservation. Their advice is *never* apply commercial or homemade furniture polishes or oils to bare wood or painted surfaces. Oils attract dust to the object and significantly darken the surface over time, altering a once finely painted surface into a aggregate of muted, undefined paint strokes. Oils are ruinous, yet many use them!

Wax. Actually, it is not necessary to put anything on the surface of a shelved decoy. The axiom *less is more* applies. However, conservators advise that it is permissible to wax a clean decoy, but only if the surface paint is stable. The wax will brighten the colors and protect against dirt and dust penetration. Light waxing should be done no more than once a year and removed with paint thinner whenever it dulls. However, buffing the wax puts pressure on the decoy surface, which may not be wise in the case of delicate birds.

Varnish. This has its pros and cons. A very thin coat could help adhere dry, loose paint back onto the wood. However, once aged, varnish becomes very difficult, if not impossible, to remove. Heat, light, and oxidation cause chemical reactions which bond the varnish to the paint. Hardened varnish is often hard and shiny to the eye and it alters the paint as it ages.

Humidity and Light

When considering care and maintenance, the two most important aspects are preserving a stable humidity level and protecting painted surfaces from ultraviolet rays from both natural and fluorescent light (this can cause paint color to fade).

Shelburne Museum decoys shelved and gently lighted behind protective glass.

humidity (or expands with increased moisture); it breaks up and flakes.

Ideally, wooden artifacts should be protected from extreme changes in both temperature and humidity. Hot weather, dry or humid, prompts us to open windows or turn on an air conditioner. During cold weather, dry air from central heating can be pervasive. Since most homes do not maintain a constant temperature and humidity level year-round, how can we protect our wooden items?

You could consider keeping your collections in one room or area which would be easy to monitor. A home which can be separated into temperature zones, each controlled by its own thermostat, would allow the temperature in the collection area to remain as constant as possible year-round. Anyone building a home, an addition, or simply remodeling can purchase a zonal heat control system. Humidifiers and/or dehumidifiers could help equalize moisture fluctuations. They are inexpensive and readily available. Even the use of glass display cases can help protect your collection.

Your home might contain many different types of collections, including china, coins, textiles, paintings, prints, furniture, as well as decoys. Painted wooden objects need special heat/moisture control. Displaying them in a separate controlled setting will protect them and prolong their existence.

Repair and Restoration

Decoys which exhibit flaking paint, dry rot, or termite or ant infestation are in a state of active deterioration. Decoys with broken bills, necks, and tails or shot scars and body checks are in static disrepair. These decoys need immediate attention if they are to be preserved. Some collectors have their lures professionally restored according to the worth of the bird and their own desire. Some prefer to keep their decoys as is while others like to see them preserved first, and then returned to near-new condition.

According to experts, fluctuating humidity will, over time, destroy painted wooden surfaces. Low relative humidity is the worst condition because dry air sucks the moisture out of wood which then shrinks or cracks. Paint cannot move when wood shrinks in low

The paint on this Canda goose by John Blair had already been totally restored when offered at auction.

If a decoy is falling apart, it deserves to be rescued! If the decoy has little value, then simple repair measures would be preferable to decay. If, however, the decoy is noteworthy, then no knowledgeable collector would prefer to see a treasured historical item disintegrate rather than be preserved by careful and expert restoration. Many people can do simple repairs; more complicated restorations should be left to experts. See Appendix A for a list of those who have experience with decoys.

Cataloging

Keep a Record

There are two important reasons for organizing and recording information about your collection. First, any insurance company will need complete data on each item you insure with them under a special coverage policy. Second, making a chronicle of each and every item, even more extensively than any insurance company would require, preserves the history of each decoy. Who made it? When and where was it made? What makes it unique? Who owned it over the years? Was it ever repaired or restored? Simply put, each decoy deserves to be remembered correctly. Also, we need to protect treasures from the irritating and often shameless influx of reproductions and outright fakes. Each item in a collection needs to be completely cataloged concerning its provenance, history, and condition. A description accompanied by a photo or videotape should be included, as well as any published information related to your collection. Catalog any pertinent information.

Provenance. Every object should have documentation relating to its provenance (origin or source). Origin, according to Webster is ''the thing from which something is ultimately derived, and often the cause in operation before the thing is brought into being.'' Most longtime collectors have gained a perspective and great respect for the historical significance of the decoy. Even so, very few of them have fully documented their ducks. Most collectors try to *remember* all they've learned, and eventu-

MR-30

DESCRIPTION: Hooded Merganser by Samuel Hutchings (1894-   ).
Elgin, Ontario, Canada. Small solid bodied-lure with "open hood" and
relief carved wings. The body is completely checkered by the use of
the sharp edge of a file. Glass eyes. Original paint. Made 1908-1914.
Size: 12" L X 4" W X 6" H. Carved diamond on top of billtip.
Identification stamped on bottom: MR-30.
Original weight and leather on bottom.
CONDITION: Excellent in body and paint.

PROVENANCE: Bernard Gates, Ontario, Canada. 1983.
                Gene and Linda Kangas, Ohio.

HISTORY: Hutchings made a few decoys between 1908 and 1914, but only
mergansers and goldeneyes. He didn't make decoys again until about 40 years
later. See: Decoys: A North American Survey by Kangas/Kangas.
Ontario Decoys by B. Gates.

EXHIBITIONS AND PUBLICATIONS:
1st Place 1984 Second Annual Toronto Decoy Show Old Decoy Contest.
Ontario Decoys II by B. Gates. page 11.
Decoys by Gene and Linda Kangas, 1991.
Collector's Guide to Decoys, Gene and Lina Kangas, 1992.

FOLK • ART

Example of a record-keeping form utilized for decoys and other folk art.

ally valuable biographical, custodial, and anecdotal material simply gets lost. Often basic information (such as origin) is lost over the years, especially as ducks are passed from person to person and generation to generation. We are the caretakers, and with that temporary ownership comes a responsibility.

The provenance document should accompany the decoy whenever it passes to a new owner—even when sold at auction.

This record provides authenticity when early data is lacking. Through the listing of all known previous owners, one can fulfill the needs of documentation, and even authenticate the document itself if it seems questionable in any respect. The complete names and addresses of previous owners, the dates of their ownership, and the dates the decoy passed to subsequent people should be listed.

Back in the early 1970s, a picker/dealer specializing in decoys found a wonderful group of late nineteenth-century scoters in a house in Maine. However, he wasn't able to purchase all the birds; so in order to sell the ones he had without divulging information as to his sources, he bestowed on them the fictitious name of Hans Berry. The decoys were bought and sold numerous times during the following decade. They were pictured in magazines, books and auction catalogs, often with Hans Berry listed as the maker. To many, Berry became the maker. Others recognized and knew the decoys as the early work of the famous Maine carver, Gus Wilson. Interestingly, in a Richard Oliver auction catalog, the picker related the story of the misattribution and cleared the record and the decoy world of the name Hans Berry—a name which had flitted around in decoy literature for nearly twenty years.

Israel Sack, prominent New York antiques dealer, once said that he would consider priceless an item of fine quality which also had interest and an absolutely authentic history. This is not to say that every quality antique with a history is priceless in itself, but such documentation affords the piece an invaluable place in history and in collections. Many dealers do not bother to document their purchases. It takes time, may interfere with their sources of merchandise, and many just wish to turn over merchandise into dollars. However, the quality level of their business, their subsequent reputation among other dealers and collectors, and the dollars they earn per year could be increased by documentation. Of course, not every item handled will come with information; but when possible, every effort should be made by collectors and dealers to gather it together and pass it on. Most people find this a rewarding pastime.

History. When known, specific data on the maker, his primary occupation, his style as it relates to other decoy carvers in his locale, and how the decoys of his region were unique should be part of the history of each item. All of this background highlights the importance and uniqueness of a particular piece.

Also included in the history should be a list of any decoy similar to yours (made by the same person or factory) which appeared in books, magazines, show or sale catalogs, and in any exhibition. The fact that these decoys are in print can help authenticate your collection in the eyes of an insurance company representative or prospective buyer. Also, if similar objects were listed in auction catalogs with their eventual sales price, this would provide some reference for valuation.

Exhibitions and Publications. A record of these can be important when dealing with the loss of an item. We all know the surprise we feel when an antique which is out of our field of study is sold or offered at a very high price. Certainly, we can understand the incredulity of an insurer's representative, especially one who doesn't specialize in fine arts. However, each company has personnel with knowledge of the general prices of antiques of many types. If an appraisal seems either too high or too low on any item, they might question you. In this case, listing every publication in which specific items appear can help validate your decoy. If the item is referred to in print, is shown on TV, or is pictured anywhere—note it. This material is an important part of the decoy's history.

Condition. All information as to wear, replacements, restoration and the extent and quality of each should be detailed. It is imperative that any restoration be documented to preserve the integrity of the piece.

Description. Decoys should be identified and differentiated from similar ones. A detailed list of characteristics should include the species of decoy, gender (drake or hen), maker, and date and place of origin, if known. The size, color, style and any patent dates, signatures, marks, stamps or brands which appear on the decoy must be noted.

Photographs. The final touch to a superb job of documentation is a clear 3″ × 5″ photo affixed to the provenance sheet. Your insurance company may not require the photo, but it's a good idea to have it. A photo provides a visual image to go with the description, and prospective buyers can be sent the provenance sheet along with the photo.

Arrange to have a good, clean, uncluttered picture of each individual item. When the scene is set up, use a plain background with no other objects. You are trying to document your decoy, not your coffee table, couch, rug, or favorite chair. Fill the photo with the duck, make sure there is plenty of light, and take more than one exposure.

Video recorders are an ideal tool with which to document. You can film a cursory view of your home including all objects to prove you own the one you're documenting. Paperwork and photographs can then back up the tape. However, the recorder can thoroughly describe each object owned as well as personal indications of identification.

If you have your collection insured adequately, but not documented thoroughly, you

Overpaint on this elegant Maine eider can be professionally tested to determine if it can be removed easily to reveal the original.

must ultimately prove its value if and when it comes time to collect. However, a complete provenance will help prove your claim. These records should be kept in a place safe from fire.

One copy could be kept at home and a second at a relative's home or in a safety deposit box. Preserve history and protect your investments. Document your decoys!

Protection

Insurance

Most people insure their home and its contents; therefore, part or all of their collectibles are possibly covered. Other people live in rental situations; and since the building owner has insurance, sometimes elect less than adequate coverage. Everyone should have protection for his possessions—furniture, clothing, and of course collectibles.

It is in your best personal and financial interests not to procrastinate about insuring your collection. Those who are just beginning to accumulate this particular kind of wealth are actually in a good position to begin to document and then insure. It doesn't require much time to coordinate the information for a small collection, and insurance premiums should be minimal. But whatever the time and premium involved, a wise collector will invest in them.

If you have a collection, you have an investment. You have consciously decided to purchase items to live with rather than put that money into a savings account or into other "paper worlds." Your investment sits on your floor, your tables, or hangs on your walls. A good collection normally accrues its own interest with time, which may be greater than that earned in a bank. It is not necessarily subject to the same inflationary variations of buying power as dollars or bonds, nor to the failure of banking institutions or the frequent fluctuations of the stock market.

Disasters. All collectibles are subject to theft, fire, breakage and other hazards. Each month notices appear in antiques journals and newspapers which list stolen items. Every new TV or appliance added to your home increases the chances of electrical overload, malfunctions and subsequent fires, not to mention fires caused by carlessness and arson. The increase of eccentric weather patterns has grown in recent years bringing floods, tornados, and other extreme conditions. Are you protected against potential loss or damage to your antiques? Can you be sure that other people in your condominium or apartment building will be as careful with fire as you are?

Most large collections have very limited protection under a general homeowner's insurance policy. One insurance adjustor related a story concerning a woman who had only one family heirloom—a beautiful antique table valued at approximately $2,000. Unfortunately, she lost it in a fire. Her homeowner's policy allowed the table to be replaced, but only to the extent of a new table of similar size which her nearest department store could supply. This points out that we cannot afford to live with the fantasy that if we have only a few antiques in our homes we don't need the bother or cost of special insurance. Disasters don't always happen to "other people." People's savings, investments for the future, and perhaps old age security may be sitting unprotected in hundreds of thousands of homes in the United States alone. Remember, ask your insurance agent how many of your antiques can be covered under your existing homeowner's policy. Then, discuss insuring the others.

Standard Policy Coverage. A collector will very likely need more insurance for the protection of his collection than his standard homeowner's policy provides. For instance, guns may be protected up to a value of $1,000 in a specific homeowner's policy. However, if one has special hunting rifles, tournament firearms or collector's pieces valued higher, the additional amount would not be covered. This same policy applies to glassware, furniture, fabrics and untold other categories. There nearly always is a low limited coverage written into a general household policy. Anything over and above the amount specifically stated for a particular type of article would not be covered in case of loss. Also, general homeowner's coverage only protects items for their *utility value*, not for their historical significance and therefore higher values.

Shop around. Coverage costs vary greatly among insurance companies. One company's rates may be double the cost of another's for exactly the same collection and same type of coverage. The homeowner's own insurance company should be checked first. Companies seem more willing to add the necessary coverage for antiques for long-standing customers. However, it might also be less expensive to switch to another company if you discover an overall better coverage at lower cost. Keep in mind that insurance companies won't be overly enthusiastic about receiving new business if it includes coverage of a high value or high risk collection. Inquire around for price quotations and then try to find a quality company knowledgeable in the area of insuring fine arts. Such a company can be expected to provide suitable coverage at a reasonable rate while cooperating quickly to complete a loss claim.

Agents Who Collect. There are insurance agents who are also collectors, even those who collect decoys! Therefore, they have an appreciation of your special insurance needs and understand the complexities of collection appraisals. They are the liason between you and the insurance company, making sure the insurance underwriter comprehends the full extent of any losses you may incur. These agents are found through word of mouth. So, ask around to find a quality company whose agents know about fine arts and feel comfortable and qualified insuring them.

Fine Arts Policy. Two additions to a homeowner's insurance policy which can provide further protection for antiques and collectibles (historical and contemporary) are called a *Collector's Form* and a *Fine Arts Form*. These protect your antiques wherever they are: At your home or in a car, in the mail, or even in a motel room. You can even send antiques to museums or galleries for exhibition purposes and be completely covered to, from, and during the exhibit. The insurance company only wishes to be made aware of what specific items are lent.

One exception for some policies is that the coverage does not necessarily apply if the item is taken to an exhibition for the purpose of sale. We take our chances on that one. However, if you are sending a collectible for sale, trade, or consideration, be sure to at least insure it with the shipper.

Appraisals

Some licensed appraisers have experience only with general household or business furnishings and property. Others may be accredited and licensed antiques appraisers with a wide basic knowledge but limited scholarship in specific areas. Auctioneers are exposed to great quantities of merchandise with the added benefit of observing the buying appetites of collectors and dealers. However, they cannot have knowledge in every specialty. According to several insurance adjusters, any person well-recognized in a specialty field may appraise and authenticate a collection. What kind of people are well-recognized? They could be respected and knowledgeable long-time active collectors, dealers, authors, and specialty auctioneers. Actually, most collectors, dealers, and authors are specialists within a specialty. In order words, they may collect and know a great deal about, say, east coast decoys and much less about birds from other regions. Major decoy auction houses, however, are usually well-versed in values from every area. It is important to discover an appraiser's expertise as well as his personal and business ethics. Put a great deal of thought into the selection of the appraiser and make certain that the appraiser will be satisfactory to your insurance company by confering with your agent.

What Is Your Purpose? There are a number of ways for an appraiser to evaluate each collection. Quite a few price levels exist on any given collectible, such as original purchase price, wholesale price to a dealer, full retail to a collector, and auction prices. Collectors may choose to insure their collections either at its full appraisal value or for less (in order to keep costs down). The collector and appraiser must decide on the type of appraisal desired.

Collections can be appraised at a high, low, or medium price range with perfectly legitimate reasons for each. You must decide what best suits your needs. You may be planning to sell soon and want to know the potential top dollar price you could reasonably expect; you may want information on value if you're making up a will.

People utilize insurance in different ways. One collector might choose to insure for full appraisal value and re-evaluate that value every couple years in view of fluctuating market prices. Another will insure his items for the original purchase price, maybe adding a few percent each year. This person is protecting basic dollar investment while keeping his insurance premiums under control. In the first instance, the collector is protecting for appreciated values including a returned investment should an item or whole collection be lost. For up-to-date accuracy, appraisers may consider auction prices over the past six to twelve months across the country as well as prices set at quality shows by established dealers. In the second instance, a record exists that demonstrates what people have recently paid in certain regions of the country at auction. Another method is to insure for the asking price by dealers (remember that they don't always get what they ask for). When insuring a collection at this level, you will pay higher insurance premiums.

One way to help minimize the cost of insurance would be to fully insure only the best objects at their highest value. Any lesser items could be insured at what was paid for them, at a minimum value, or perhaps not insured at all. Your best bet would be to fully protect your collection while retaining some control of soaring insurance costs. This can be a good idea. However, if the whole collection is lost through theft or fire, a lot of investment dollars could also be lost. Each collector must decide how the investment is to be viewed. Does the collection represent his savings? If so, one must make sure money isn't thrown away due to loss. One person will want every dollar of investment and growth fully covered by the insurance, another will decide to take out general coverage, and, of course, some will never decide anything at all.

Every collector who owns a home is quick to insure it. Depending where they live, most collectors who own a car have some insurance on it. They know the banks insure their savings, and life insurance is always deemed a necessity. Isn't your collection just as important?

No-Cost Safeguards

In addition to insurance, there are other ways you can safeguard your collection.

Become a more cautious person. Don't advertise that there are fascinating items in your home. This means that you shouldn't invite salesmen or repairmen to tour your house and admire your collection. *Avoid publicity.* Don't encourage articles to appear in local newspapers which might indicate by word or photograph that there are desirable antiques behind your doors. *Lock your doors and windows before you go to bed and when you leave the house.* Certainly you've heard true stories of thieves slipping into a sleeping household and making off with the goodies without anyone waking. Homes have been looted through the front door while the family was tending the garden or playing ball in the backyard. *Leave lights and a radio turned on while you are out. Keep extra house keys to a minimum.* Above all, don't hide keys outside the house for emergencies. You'd be better off giving one to a trusted neighbor than putting one out for an enterprising burglar.

Low-Cost Safeguards

The truth is that most thieves steal those things they understand and can readily turn into money. Few people know the value of and where to get money for the range of items that people collect. Therefore, if your home is a potential robbery target, the things most likely to be taken will be the old standbys: televisions, camcorders, VCRs, money, jewelry, coins, and guns! But decoys? One of the saddest stories in the decoy fraternity centers around the burglary of the home of one of America's well-known decoy collecting couples. While they were on vacation many years ago, their home was robbed and many things were taken including family heirlooms and memories, but not the decoys. What did the intruders do upon encountering so many unfamiliar objects? They broke them. A heart-breaking scene for the couple when they returned.

One of the most common defenses used is to arrange for a reliable person to live in your home whenever you're going to be away for several days or weeks. Collectors might contact a young married couple or a conscientious college student for this job. Someone needs to actually stay at the house, not just pop in and out for spot checks. Dogs are a deterrent, too. Large or small, they all bark. Thieves tend to stay away from homes with dogs.

The Alarm System

Our friends, the robbery victims, would probably advise other collectors to do what they finally did: Install an alarm system and use it faithfully day and night.

Break-in alarm systems, medical alerts, and smoke and fire detector combinations can range from several hundred to several thousand dollars installed. You can choose a "home only" warning system or one that can be hooked up directly to a monitoring company for a small monthly fee. Using the sophisticated and relatively inexpensive equipment available, a monitoring company can read the status of your alarm system, determine whether you have a break-in, fire, or medical emergency and call the appropriate personnel quicker than you could. For under $2,000, you can have all this protection twenty-four hours a day, 365 days a year. It's a prudent way to spend a moderate sum of money. If you don't have the ready cash, you can lease a system. You might want to consider selling one or two items to afford the alarm system so that the rest of the collection will be better protected. Or, when you have saved enough money to add to your collection, this time buy an alarm system instead.

CHAPTER ELEVEN

The Art of Modern Wildfowl Carving

History

A brief survey of the history of decoy-generated wildlife art provides a microcosmic view of the logical evolution of this native art form. Working with natural materials, prehistoric North American Indians created the first hunting decoys. Later, immigrant hunters and trappers adopted the idea and began developing the once ephemeral Indian decoy into more permanent wooden lures. The many varied individuals carving and hunting in their own geographical regions ultimately helped establish recognizable regional styles which directly correspond to local hunting methods based on water conditions, food sources, species of birds, flyway locations, and laws. Regional styles were also influenced by social circumstances.

From each conglomeration of regional design characteristics arose carvers acknowledged as the best. Their talents successfully combined functional elements along with their own personal touch to create classic prototypical decoys. The names of these long-recognized greats are a part of decoy history in need of additional research. It must be as-

sumed that each carver took pride in his creations.

These carvers have been consistently categorized as folk artists; however, incorrect assumptions have been expressed that they worked alone—almost in a vacuum. Evidence indicates that a broad range of worldly influences existed.

The first decoy exhibition was the 1923 Bellport, New York show which is recognized as a transitional point in decoy carving history. Competition between individuals became a new incentive which ultimately transformed the look of traditionally based lures. Each new set of show judges brought with them their own preferential aesthetics and criteria which became factors affecting the design and look of competition birds. Joel Barber, the 1923 show organizer and premier collector of the time, soon recognized the influence shows were having on carvers. Decoys were being created for the aesthetics of men rather than purely to attract ducks. However, decoys had already been changed by other factors before that time.

During the late 19th and early 20th centuries, there were a variety of other influences on decoys. Academic artists of the time painted and carved popular sporting scenes of such realism that people often mistook them for live birds. This artwork, or copies thereof, was published in books and hung in private and public establishments and greatly admired by all. Businessmen of the time had both the money and leisure to pursue arts and sporting activities. They traveled the continent spreading their ideal aesthetics far and wide.

Such a traveling hunter, visiting game areas in Louisiana, might have influenced the look of today's Louisiana decoys. In *Louisiana Duck Decoys*, author Charles Frank questioned carver Mitchel LaFrance about influences on paint patterns and received this startling answer: ''Why,'' LaFrance replied promptly, ''some sportsman brought a book to the senior George Frederick [a relative and carving partner of LaFrance] with the request that a certain design be copied for him on a dozen decoys. So they copied it; the origin was as simple as that. Magically, a demand for the new pattern developed and spread.'' These imported patterns resemble traditional Illinois River styles. This illustrates how easily outside sources might alter an area's aesthetics. The possibilities for interaction between artist, art patron, sportsman, hunter, guide and carver are obviously numerous. The influences that each might have had on the other are important and merit investigation.

It was during the early 1900s that some decoy carvers, completely of their own initiative, turned their hands to elaborate nonworking renditions of their own styling, when they had the time or encouragement to do so. Decoratives were born by a few creative decoy makers such as Elmer Crowell, Ira Hudson, Shang Wheeler and the Ward Brothers who, although working separately, created lifelike sculptural bird carvings not duplicated by the masses until nearly fifty years later. They pursued these directions because of creative urges and because of financial reward.

The fledgling Competitive Show Era begun in the 1920s manifested new decoy concerns. As carvers spent more and more time preparing decoys for exhibition, the production of actual hunting blocks began to be replaced by mantle birds. The years spanning the early 1920s to the mid-1960s might be referred to as the period of The Mantle Decoy or The Show Decoy. The development and dissemination of new tools and techniques excited carvers who soon reinvented truly nonfunctional and highly decorative waterfowl decoys. They advanced the models to again fool the eye as had been done before the turn of the century by the academicians. A new period of The Decorative Decoy came to be in the mid-1960s. Carvers aspired to create a feather-covered wooden bird that appeared to breathe. Although these highly decorative and realistic birds seem a distant relative to the first working decoys, they share a lineage of technical improvements and aesthetic changes.

Modern Wildfowl Carvers

Today, a variety of new paths are being explored by contemporary carvers that go considerably beyond past and recent tradition. Carvers are beginning to think of themselves as artists and sculptors. The larger art world poses new challenges; it demands that new forms of expression be constantly expanded. Change is important. In order for fine artists to establish their mark in the history of art they must forge new paths—paths of quality and merit. They must become leaders, not followers. An art critic might raise the question that if modern wildfowl carvers are able to craft birds that are so lifelike they seem to come alive and make you smile with pleasure, why can't they also tackle more pressing social and ecological issues? If one carving can elicit laughter, shouldn't another one be able to touch your heart and bring tears to your eyes? Would such emotionally loaded expressions be accepted by competition judges? Could they win? Would the collecting public financially support such works of art? As aesthetics continue to slowly change and evolve, and new contest categories are introduced, the answer is *yes*. In fact, several carvers have already begun pushing the boundaries of traditional wildfowl carving.

The following individuals represent a small cross section of the numerous carving styles practiced today. Their ideas are but a few of the many that are being explored throughout North America by the new generation of artist/craftsman whose roots are tied by each preceding generation to the original decoy makers. They are learning from the past and are using updated information each in their own style.

Dave and Mary Ahrendt of Hackensack, Minnesota, are a husband and wife carving/painting team. He carves, she paints. The two collaborate on ideas and have developed a recognizable style since turning professional in 1983. They describe their work as an "impressionistic use of natural wood with realistic focal points." For example, in walnut sculptures like *Peregrine Falcon and Cliff Swallow*, the heads of each bird were typically rendered in realistic detail while other body parts were simplified and intentionally distorted and blurred to suggest speed.

Dave and Mary begin by first discussing ideas and then sketching them on paper. Clay models and small carvings then follow to solve various problems. Larger pieces are roughed out with a chain saw and finished with an assortment of tools. The Ahrendts indicate that there appears to be a movement towards

Peregrine Falcon and Cliff Swallow by David & Mary Ahrendt. Walnut painted with acrylics, 40″ × 25″ × 20″.

more sculptural forms and a decline in emphasis on pure technical facility. To paraphrase famous early twentieth-century academic sculptor Constantin Brancusi, "When you see a fish swimming, you don't see the fish in detail; you only see the essence or spirit of the fish." The Ahrendts are attempting to capture and portray the spirit of their avian subjects.

Don Briddell of Mt. Airy, Maryland, first learned to carve by working for the famous Ward Brothers of Crisfield, Maryland, from 1957 to 1962. It was, therefore, natural that his first years would include both working and decorative carvings of merit. His art has evolved considerably since that time, and his following comments indicate Don's current attitudes toward carving. "Now that we all know what a bird looks like, we will be putting that knowledge to use creating larger statements. Now that we know how to spell, we will attempt to make sentences and then write whole books with our new sense of realism and the meaningful. Art will become a bigger issue than 'look alike' realism. The public will have to grow with the artist in this regard. The potential is for the field to become a major movement in American art history, but only if *art* becomes more of an issue than realism. I feel we are on the verge of a new, higher level of involvement. We are intellectually, if not emotionally, ready."

Two very different Briddell sculptures, *Leonardo* and *Homeplate*, portray both Don's abilities as a carver and his openness to explore new areas. *Leonardo* was carved in 1983 and represents, in Don's words, a traditional carving policy of "attempting to carve a highly detailed and complex form from a single block of wood without insertions." This drake mallard, however, does have bronze feet. By

Leonardo by Don Briddell. Life-size mallard drake made from one piece of wood with attached bronze feet, 1983. Basswood and acrylics.

Homeplate, barn swallows wall hanging sculpture by Don Briddell. Cast resin birds with wood and antique license plate, 1989, 24″ × 42″ × 5″.

contrast, the wall sculpture, *Homeplate*, was designed from several high- and low-tech materials. Each was chosen for a specific purpose. Resins, wood and an antique license plate were the primary materials used. Art should not be bound by media; rather ideas should determine what an artist does.

Tan, Jude and Jett Brunet are a carving family from Louisiana. Tan started carving as a teenager. He was greatly influenced by Jimmy Vizier, his father Odee, and his uncle Clovis "Cadis" Vizier. His earliest efforts were working decoys with a Louisiana heritage. Since then, Tan has helped pioneer the evolution from working decoy to decoratives in his area. His sons have followed successfully in the family tradition. (It is satisfying to know that family traditions continue even in

today's high-tech society. Good role models are important.)

Commenting for himself as well as Jude and Jett, Tan tells us: "We buy the raw wood and sketch the patterns right on the block. We make birds in one piece. We first rough them with a hatchet; and next we use rasps, knives and texturing machines, then burning irons and then artist oils." He indicated that shows and judges are beginning to lean toward artistic freedom and are more open to birds displayed in flamboyant poses.

Habbart Dean lives in Bishopville, Maryland. He started carving in 1979; since then he has completed a broad range of waterfowl, songbirds and shorebirds. Habbart carves both lifesize and miniature decoratives. Each species is approached with an open mind concerning depiction and presentation. A comparison of *Red-Breasted Merganser* and *Black Skimmers* illustrates this point. The merganser directly reflects its "decoy ancestors" while the skimmers are closely linked to more contemporary trends.

In answer to our question about what sort of role the competitions and shows play, Habbart commented, "Major—they offer the opportunity for carvers to compare their work with that of their peers. At 'The World' [the

Red-breasted Merganser by Habbart Dean. Carved and painted wood.

Left to right: Tan Brunet, Jimmy Vizier, Jett Brunet and Jude Brunet holding their prize winners.

Black Skimmers by Habbart Dean. Carved and painted wood.

annual Ward World Championships held in Ocean City, Maryland] we have attempted to develop standards and categories, i.e. Interpretive Sculpture, to encourage 'breaking out.' ''

Pat Godin of Paris, Ontario, has been successfully carving waterfowl since 1972. In 1979 he received an advanced degree from the University of Guelph where he specialized in avian biology. His indepth knowledge of waterfowl habits and anatomy have been put to practice. He says, ''Because I have become recognized for such decoy-style carvings, the demand from collectors is greatest for these as opposed to other full-bodied decorative bird carvings. Over the last several years, my decorative decoys have gradually become more complex in design. In some cases, I have at-tempted to capture a moment when the bird is very active; this results in highly animated carvings. To successfully create such complex pieces, I initially work out the design in clay before beginning to work in wood. Despite this evolution in my own work from relatively simply designed decoys to complex works, I firmly believe that more complexity does not necessarily make a better carving. Most important, regardless of the level of complexity, is to capture the character and attitude of the real bird and to incorporate aspects of design that are aesthetically pleasing to a viewer. I believe that most of the creators of antique decoys instinctively had these same goals.''

Godin's *Red-Breasted Merganser Pair* represents well the concept of a decorative decoy. Each is a singular portrait that imitates

Red-breasted Merganser Pair by Pat Godin, 1989. Carved and painted wood.

Pintail Drake by Pat Godin, 1991. Carved and painted wood.

the interaction and antics of shelldrakes on the water. *Pintail Drake*, however, is a much more complicated portrait. The amount of body posturing, highly raised feathers and other anatomical elaborations is far distant from the original idea of a working decoy. In fact, Godin feels that "Today's best decorative decoy carvings have reached such a level of technical refinement that one can only expect miniscule and trivial improvements in the future. It is not likely that wood can be burned any finer than it has been. Several carvers have learned to paint light and shadow very convincingly and to create incredible illusions of feather translucency with their opaque painting media. Carvers near the top of the field have generally realized that progress in the art form lies in creativity of design and in communicating innovative concepts, not in more refinement of detail. By this I do not necessarily mean more complexity of design, but unique ideas." It will be interesting to see how Pat Godin is able to combine these thoughts with his background knowledge and technical expertise to create exciting new wildfowl portraits in the near future.

Road Runner and Lizard by William J. Koelpin. Carved and painted wood.

William Koelpin is a well-rounded artist who lives in Hartland, Wisconsin. Bill started carving working decoys for his own use at an early age. This activity, however, quickly evolved into decorative carving as well as expressions with oil-on-canvas and bronze. He states that, ''In some respects, we have lost the early [Ira Hudson era] interpretive efforts of depicting wildfowl, which I think were more creative. The living bird has become the criteria instead of the creative individual interpretation.''

Pair of Greater Prairie Chickens and *Road Runner and Lizard* are two carvings which demonstrate Koelpin's attention to realism and perfection. Each subject is well researched prior to sculpting. In addition, statements in oil and bronze reflect his duck hunter heritage. Humor and nostalgia are both evident in two-dimensional images such as *Fowl Tip, Damn the Wind*, and *Good Times*. William Koelpin has demonstrated the ability to expand his artistic vocabulary from decoy making to fine art.

Pair of Greater Prairie Chickens by William J. Koelpin. Carved and painted wood.

Leo Osborne from Joseph, Oregon, creates intriguing and expressive sculptures from burl, other woods, and various materials. The two burl works illustrated, *Brothers of the Wood* and *Still Not Listening*, express very different attitudes about Leo's personal thoughts of nature and society. His comments are noteworthy. "I am a free-spirited sculptor who strives to be at the leading edge. While I was working on *Still Not Listening*, the oil spill in Prince William Sound, Alaska, happened as I was two-thirds of the way into sculpting. I was so moved by this catastrophe that I finished the first bird on its back and then planned to engulf it in an oil-like substance; the second bird feeding and about to get caught in it; and the third bird doing a warlike Indian dance with wings outstretched. I dedicated the act of sculpting the piece to Prince William Sound."

After completing the carving and sanding this lovely piece of beautiful birdseye maple wood, I took a caulking gun, most symbolic, and squirted black vinyl caulking over its surface. This became, to me, a feeling of destruction of beauty. It reminded me a great deal of the 'happenings' of the 1960s when artists would demonstrate, through creative means and portrayals, what was taking place in the world of mankind. I do not choose to keep creating these blatant statements of environmental destruction but concentrate on creating pieces that depict symbolic statements of wildlife and social and environmental actions—changes that are necessary for life to continue and grow in spirit and grace!"

Leo is currently involved with creating a series of relief wall sculptures—stonelike ledges with pictographs of ancient scenes and figures combined with shadows of animals walking and/or flying across the panorama of

Brothers of the Wood, wolf and raven by Leo E. Osborne, 1991, 36″ diameter maple birdseye burl.

these surfaces. Often endangered species are portrayed in these shadowed images. The series is entitled *Watching my Brothers Pass*, and thus far has incorporated wolves, ravens, bison, big horn sheep, elephants, kukus, and eagles.

Leo Osborne is proving to be a thinking, caring citizen who is choosing to direct his artistic talents to help make the world a better place to live. A risk taker, he was willing to subject a beautiful carving made from a beautiful piece of wood to a covering of sludge to make a point. He is a competitor at "The World" level, but his vision is not constrained by rules and regulations.

Dennis Schroeder is a full-time carver who lives in North Fork, California. He studied art in school and began carving in 1983 after attending a wildfowl carving competition. A lot of hard work has resulted in considerable success since then. His work refers back to the idea of a decoy but with new attitudes and approaches. According to Dennis, his philosophy is "to create a lifelike carving, giving each piece that spark which brings the bird to life, in an attitude or pose that is both pleasing and interesting. Special effort is made to capture the essence of each individual species. All birds are thoroughly researched, by extensive photography sessions in lake and marshland areas and in my own aviary where I keep a large selection of waterfowl. All carvings are

Still Not Listening by Leo E. Osborne.

American Wigeons by Dennis Schroeder. Carved and painted wood.

Mute Swans by Dennis Schroeder. Carved and painted wood.

created from a single block of tupelo wood; no separate heads or inserts are used. They are then hand-painted in oils. No patterns are used, and each piece is an original design."

Wigeon Pair and *Mute Swans* illustrate his decoy roots. Dennis prefers carving waterfowl in the traditional style with flat bottoms and feels that "the mind will perceive them as swimming, even without habitat being added." His thoughts for the future are considering "increased finish work and creating interesting artistic poses."

John T. Sharp from Kent, Ohio, is another accomplished and outspoken carver who has evolved his own distinct style. He tends to work on a life-size scale reducing sections of hardwood logs to the avian images within. Training as an industrial model and pattern maker has provided him with an extensive knowledge of tools and materials. John feels that, "the significance of the work being done

by the relatively few people carving life-size birds from one piece of wood, is that their styles are individualistic and widely varied ac-

Mallard Jumping by John T. Sharp, 1983. Black walnut, 22" diameter × 20" high.

Canvasback by John T. Sharp, 1986. Black walnut, 20″ × 32″ × 12″.

cording to their own vision and skills.'' Commenting on juried competitions, he says: ''I do not believe that competition serves art. When accuracy of subject matter is the criterion, everyone is working to the same end, i.e., the highest degree of realism. Individual style is denied except for technique.''

Sharp's waterfowl images interact in environmental settings that seem to emerge naturally out of hardwood logs. They are expressions of living forms that reflect their origins. The elegance of his unpainted sculptures is based upon a universal understated beauty. Less is more.

Barton Walter lives in Westminster, Maryland. His original interest in decoy carving grew out of his boyhood passion for duck hunting. Although he set out to make his own rig of decoys, he was somehow sidetracked into a career of decorative bird carving. Reflecting on his interest in old decoys, Bart raises the concerns of many contemporary

Defiance by Barton Walter, 1989. Broad-winged hawk, 18″ tall.

Marsh King by Barton Walter, 1983. Great Blue Heron, six feet tall.

far more important than absolute anatomical accuracy. In my work today, I try very hard indeed to incorporate principles of art/sculpture in order to breathe life into my carvings. I guess you could say my emphasis is now on form and design, rather than on technique or details."

Defiance and *Marsh King* represent two sculptural works which illustrate these attitudes. It is important to realize that while technique and media are integral aspects of art, they must follow the dictates of one's ideas.

Todd Wohlt is presently living in New London, Wisconsin. Interestingly, Todd started carving at age twelve when he helped repair old decoys his grandfather hunted over. Those were August Moak canvasbacks. He graduated to making his own hunting decoys and eventually became fascinated with decorative carvings. Besides ducks, he carves many bird species and tries to keep his work "fresh and innovative and to do something different."

Dive! typifies that conviction. It is a narrative scene depicting a life-size black duck swimming in hot pursuit of a fleeing pied-billed grebe. The grebe is firmly holding onto a crab claw as it speeds away.

Todd begins a carving by first spending time observing the antics of live birds. Then he creates full-size scale models and makes necessary changes in preparation to approaching the wood. For the future, he envisions "simple, elegant poses and designs with super-realistic painted surfaces." Of course, that does not take into account observances of unexpected occurrences in nature. New sights might stimulate new ideas.

The transition that occurred from early waterfowl decoys to today's sophisticated wildfowl portraits was a slow process spanning over a century. A complex mixture of influences, technical advancements and personalities has brought us to the present. You can begin collecting or carving today.

carvers when he observes: "Competitions are becoming less popular with many carvers as attention shifts away from technical accuracy and more towards the intangibles of good art. How do you judge a Lee Dudley against an Elmer Crowell; and if you do, is it fair? Several years ago, I set out to learn more about sculpture and I quickly realized what the great old decoy makers of a century ago seemed to know intuitively; that capturing the essence of your subject in your own form of shorthand is

Dive! by Todd Wonit, 1990. Black duck chases a pied-billed grebe.

The carvers profiled represent only a few of the thousands currently practicing. Their combined comments suggest an uneasiness with the restrictions of some competitions if categories reflect only a repetitive technical look at wildlife. Indications are that the once purely functional decoy has metamorphasized into an aspiring art form.

If that is the goal, then carvers must be willing to journey away from the safe and protective confines of specialty competitions and risk entering the academic art world. Some are already beginning to do that. The art community, unfortunately, is also controlled by trends, personal and aesthetic preferences,

power struggles and subjective criticism. For example, how would you expect trained academic sculptors to judge the Interpretive Wood Sculpture class if they had either a strong abstract or realistic bias? At the same time, there exists a greater latitude for expression and an openness to media possibilities. Rebellion is understood. Change is a constant. In the end, each artist must ultimately be judged exclusively on the merits of his creations. Modern wildfowl carvers are pushing their field forward. Carving competitions and shows, we're sure, will soon move as quickly as do today's energetic and explosive artists.

Collecting Modern Carvings

Many people already collect old working decoys and many others now also collect decoratives, miniatures and/or modern wildfowl carvings. Develop a plan of action. Modern carvings can be purchased at competitions and exhibitions. (See Appendix F for a listing.) Some artists don't have works available through galleries, so it is either at these shows or by contacting them at their studios that you might be able to purchase directly from them. You might acquire works on hand or commis-

sion particular pieces. At the shows and exhibitions, you can meet the artists and get to know them. Your personal relationship will add considerably to the pleasure you will receive from living with their creations.

Modern carvings can also be purchased from art galleries who represent the artists. Many advertise in national publications related to the field. The carvers profiled in this chapter indicated that, depending on the individual piece and the complexity of the work, prices for modern carvings range from a few hundred dollars to tens of thousands. It's obvious that carvings done in a few days should be much less expensive than major efforts which might consume a year or more. Modern wildfowl carvings are generally highly detailed and somewhat delicate. They should all be in mint condition and it is the collector's responsibility to maintain that condition (see Chapter Ten).

With decoys, many types of collections can be established. You might put together a grouping of your favorite carver's work, or songbirds by many carvers, or miniatures and life-size renditions of the same species, or any other preference. Having a direction is important in helping you develop the collection so that the long-term results are both pleasing to you and potentially a sound investment.

How to Begin Carving

If this book has inspired you to try your hand at wildfowl carving, here are some helpful suggestions to get you started. Pay attention to your local media for announcements of any shows that might be held in your area. You might also contact several of the specialty book dealers listed in Appendix B for lists and information on carving magazines and ''how-to'' books. There are many! Magazines usually itemize activities for the whole continent on an annual basis. Many of the successful carvers also advertise classes, instructional video tapes, and books in these publications.

At most shows, you can expect to watch practical demonstrations of various types and you can also see up close many of the carvings being entered in the contests. In most cases, you are able to observe the judging. If you are bold enough, you might be able to meet and have a good talk with any number of carvers in attendance. Shows also afford the opportunity to purchase blocks of special carving woods like clear pine, basswood and jelutong. Some dealers are usually on hand with a tremendous assortment of carving tools and painting supplies. Some offer mail order catalogs.

Museums like the Ward Foundation in Salisbury, Maryland, host carving seminars and are great sources of information. These seminars might make an interesting vacation. Contact them and join the museum to get their publications (Appendix G). Once you get started carving, it is important that you decide on the purpose and direction of your interests. Those decisions will help determine your next course of action.

Professional Restorers

Allen Bell
2347 Gerrard Street East
Toronto, Ontario, Canada M4E 2E6
Telephone 416-698-0126

Ken Delong
Pinewood Road
Hyannis, Massachusetts 02601
Telephone 508-775-5928

William Feasel
1810 Finley Drive
Fremont, Ohio 43420
Telephone 419-334-2845 or
419-334-7844

Frank Finney
1909 Indian River Road
Virginia Beach, Virginia 23456
Telephone 804-426-7242

William Hanemann
302 Fountain Street
Mandeville, Louisiana 70448
Telephone 504-624-8213

Gigi Hopkins
5 H Iris Court
Acton, Massachusetts 01720
Telephone 508-369-8720

Valerie Hunt Reich
Professionally Trained Conservator
Shelburne Museum
Rt. 7
Shelburne, Vermont 05482
Telephone 802-985-3346

Gene Kangas
Artist, Sculptor, Restorer
P.O. Box 609
Concord, Ohio 44077
Telephone 216-352-5321

Cameron McIntyre
P.O. Box 12
Assawoman, Virginia 23302-9998
Telephone 804-824-5125

John G. Percy
Morristown
Ontario, Canada
Telephone 519-837-3753

Specialty Book Dealers

All of the books listed in Appendix C can be purchased from the following book dealers:

Paul Brisco
49 Bromleigh Avenue
London, Ontario, Canada N6G 1V1
Telephone: 519-641-4790

Chestnut Ridge Books
Luke Cuccia
133 St. Joseph Boulevard
P.O. Box 731
Lodi, New Jersey 07644
Telephone: 201-282-7072

Dean and Shirley Dashner
453 Pendleton Road
Neenah, Wisconsin 54956
Telephone: 414-725-4350 or
414-725-4421

P. C. English
Box 380
Thornburg, Virginia 22565
Telephone: 703-582-2200

Henry A. Fleckenstein
Box 577
Cambridge, Maryland 21613
Telephone: 301-221-0076

Grove Decoys
Bill and Carol Bender
36 West 44th Street
New York, New York 10036
Telephone: 212-391-0688

Highwood Book Shop
Lewis Rezek
Rt. 2, Box 213
Suttons Bay, Michigan 49682
Telephone: 616-271-3898

Richard McNally
Fair Chase, Inc.
9310 402nd Avenue
Genoa City, Wisconsin 53128
Telephone: 414-279-5478

John and Marquita Staab
623 River Road
Maumee, Ohio 43537
Telephone: 419-891-1064

Books for Collectors

Refer to Appendix B for a list of suppliers from whom books can be purchased.

Barber, Joel
  Wildfowl Decoys

Berkey, Barry and Velma
  Chincoteague Carvers & Their Decoys
  Pioneer Decoy Carvers—A Biography of Lemuel and Stephen Ward
  Decoy and Wildlife Art Trivia

Brisco, Paul R.
  Waterfowl Decoys of Southwestern Ontario and the Men Who Made Them

Buckwalter, H. R.
  Susquehanna River Decoys

Burke, Patricia H.
  Barnegat Bay Decoys and Gunning Clubs

Cheever, Byron
  Mason Decoys

Chitwood, Marshall and Knight
  Connecticut Working Decoys

Colio, Quintina
  American Decoys from 1865 to 1920

Connett, Eugene V.
  Duck Shooting Along the Atlantic Tidewater
  Wildfowling in the Mississippi Flyway

Conoley, William Neal, Jr.
  Waterfowl Heritage—North Carolina Decoys & Gunning Lore

Coykendall, Ralf, Jr.
  Joel Barber's Americana (Poetry by Barber)
  Decoy Collecting

Crandall, Bernard W.
  Decoying St. Clair to St. Lawrence

Delph, John and Shirley
  Factory Decoys
  New England Decoys

Dewhurst and MacDowell
  Downriver and Thumb Area Michigan Waterfowling

Earnest, Adele
  The Art of the Decoy—American Bird Carvings

Elman, Robert
  The Atlantic Flyway

Engers, Joe, ed.
  The Great Book of Wildfowl Decoys

Fleckenstein, Henry
  American Factory Decoys
  Decoys of the Mid-Atlantic Region
  New Jersey Decoys
  Shore Bird Decoys
  Southern Decoys of Virginia & Carolinas

Fleming, Patricia
  Traditions in Wood (Canadian Decoys)

Frank, Charles W.
  Louisiana Duck Decoys
  Wetland Heritage—The Louisiana Duck Decoy

Gard and McGrath
  The Ward Brothers Decoys

Gates, Bernie
  Ontario Decoys I
  Ontario Decoys II

Gosner, Kenneth
  Working Decoys of the Jersey Coast & Delaware Valley

Guyette, Dale and Gary
  Decoys of Maritime Canada

Hagan, David and Joan
  Upper Chesapeake Bay Decoys & Their Makers

Haid, Alan
  Decoys of the Mississippi Flyway

Harrell, Loy S.
  Decoys of Lake Champlain

Holliday, Alan S.
American Decoys

Huster and Knight
Floating Sculpture—Decoys of the Delaware River

Jackson, Lowell
Ben J. Schmidt—Michigan Carver

Johnsgard, Paul
The Bird Decoy—An American Art Form

Kangas, Gene and Linda
Decoys—A North American Survey
Decoys
Collector's Guide to Decoys

Koch, Ronald M.
Decoys of the Winnebago Lakes

Levinson, John M. and Headley, Somers G.
Shorebirds: The Birds, The Hunters, The Decoys

Linton and Lawson
The Story of Lem Ward

Mackey, William
American Bird Decoys
Decoy Auction Catalogs

McKinney, J. Evans
Decoys of the Susquehanna Flats

Merkt, Dixon MacD.
Shang

Miller, Stephen M.
Early American Waterfowling: 1700s–1930

Miller and Hanson
Wildfowl Decoys of the Pacific Coast

Murphy, Stanley
Martha's Vineyard Decoys

North American Decoys
L. T. Ward & Co. Wildfowl Counterfeiters

Parmalee and Loomis
Decoys and Decoy Carvers of Illinois

Reiger, George
Floaters & Stick Ups

Richardson, R. H.
Chesapeake Bay Decoys

Ridges, Bob
Decoy Ducks

Robbins, Charles Lee
R. Madison Mitchell—His Life and Decoys

Sorenson, Hal
Decoy Collectors Guide 1963, 1964, 1965
Decoy Collectors Guide Volume 4—1966–67
Decoy Collectors Guide Volume 5—1968
Decoy Collectors Guide Volume 6—1977

Starr, George Ross
Decoys of the Atlantic Flyway

Stewart and Lunman
Decoys of the Thousand Islands

Sullivan, C. John, Jr.
Robert F. McGaw, Jr.—A Chronicle of Letters
Waterfowling—The Upper Chesapeake's Legacy

Swanson and Hall
The Decoy as Folk Sculpture

Townsend, E. J.
Gunner's Paradise: Wildfowling and Decoys on Long Island

Traff and Lindgren
Last of the Prairie Carvers, John Tax

Turnbull, Hugh
The Judas Birds—A Show of Rare Canadian and American Decoys at Musee Marsil Museum

Waingrow, Jeff
American Wildfowl Decoys

Walsh and Jackson
Waterfowl Decoys of Michigan & The Lake St. Clair Region

Warner and White
The Decoy as Art

Webster and Kehoe
Decoys of the Shelburne Museum

Magazines for Collectors

Decoy Geographer
4532 Old Leeds Road
Birmingham, Alabama 35213

Decoy Hunter
901 North 9th Street
Clinton, Indiana 47842

Decoy Magazine
P.O. Box 277
Burtonsville, Maryland 20866

North American Decoys
Hillcrest Publications
P.O. Box 246
Spanish Fork, Utah 84660

Wildfowl Arts
Journal of the Ward Foundation
P.O. Box 3416
Salisbury, Maryland 21802

Wildfowl Carving and Collecting
P.O. Box 1831
Harrisburg, Pennsylvania 17105

Appendix E
Auction Houses

Included here are auction houses that specialize in and hold waterfowl sales sometimes several times each year; they are indicated with an asterisk. Others occasionally sell decoys and other bird carvings intermixed in General or Americana sales.

*Richard A. Bourne
P.O. Box 141
Hyannis Port, Massachusetts 02647
508-775-0797

*Decoys Unlimited
Ted Harmon
2320 Main Street
West Barnstable, Massachusetts 02668
508-362-2766

Robert C. Eldred, Co., Inc.
Route 6A, P. O. Box 796
East Dennis, Massachusetts 02641
617-385-3116

Mike Fahnder's Auctions
RR 2
Pekin, Illinois 61554
309-346-0467 or
309-346-6777

Garth's Auctions, Inc.
2690 Stratford Rd., P.O. Box 369
Delaware, Ohio 43015
614-362-4771

Morton Goldberg Auction Galleries, Inc.
3000 Magazine Street
New Orleans, Louisiana 70115

*James Julia/Gary Guyette
Box 522
West Farmington, Maine 04992
207-778-6266

Robert J. Kasper
5718 W. Little Portage
Port Clinton, Ohio 43452
419-734-2930

Martindale's Decoy Works
Box 218, Wolfe Island
Ontario, Canada K0H 2Y0
613-385-2975

Merrill's Auction Gallery
Williston, Vermont 05495
802-878-2625

*Richard W. Oliver Auction Gallery
Box 337
Kennebunk, Maine 04043
207-985-3600

Phillips, Son, and Neale, Inc.
406 East 79th Street
New York, New York 10021
212-570-4830

Potter & Knight
5 Plaunt Street C
Renfrew, Ontario, Canada K7V 1M5
Tim Potter 613-386-3635
Cecil Knight 613-432-3022

Sanchez Antiques and Auction Galleries
4730 Magazine Street
New Orleans, Louisiana

Robert W. Skinner, Incorporated
357 Main Street, Bolton, Mass. 01740
2 Newbury Street, Boston, Mass. 02116
617-779-5528

Sotheby's
American Decorative Arts Department
1334 York Avenue
New York, New York 10021
212-606-7000

Sotheby's
Toronto, Ontario, Canada
416-926-1774

Waddington, McLean & Co. Ltd.
189 Queen Street E.
Toronto, Ontario, Canada M5A 1S2
416-362-1678

Clubs and Shows

There are active collecting clubs in each flyway. Some clubs host one annual show per year, others do even more with monthly meetings, picnics, and seminars. A few of them provide a membership directory and/or a club newsletter. Some clubs were organized to foster both collecting and carving, and their shows reflect both interests.

The Northeast

New England Decoy Collectors Association
Contact: Ted Harmon
Telephone: 508-362-2766

The Mid-Atlantic

Long Island Decoy Collectors Association
Babylon, New York
Contact: George Combs
Telephone: 516-264-3525

The Central Atlantic

Back Bay Wildfowl Guild
Virginia Beach, Virginia
Contact: Emma Meehan
Telephone: 804-340-5921

The South

Carolina Decoy Collectors and Carvers
   Association
Contact: Bruce Cameron
Telephone: 919-763-1054

Louisiana Wildfowl Carvers & Collectors Guild
New Orleans, Louisiana
Contact: Charles Frank
Telephone: 504-588-9143

Texas Decoy Collectors Association
Dallas, Texas
Contact: Brian McGrath
Telephone: 214-867-5980

The Midwest

Midwest Decoy Collectors Association
Chicago, Illinois

Contact: Bob Wohlers
Telephone: 402-488-6514

Minnesota Decoy Collectors Association
St. Paul, Minnesota
Contact: Dick Brust
P.O. Box 13043, St. Paul, MN 55113

Northwestern Michigan Waterfowl Decoy
   Association
Traverse City, Michigan
Contact: Jim Reynolds
Telephone: 616-271-3898

Northwood Decoy Collectors
Northern Wisconsin
Contact: Greg Guthrie
Telephone: 715-588-7626

Ohio Decoy Collectors & Carvers Association
Cleveland, Ohio
Contact: Robert Lund
Telephone: 419-874-3671

Toronto Decoy Show
Toronto, Ontario
Contact: Sam Stuart
Telephone: 416-644-3158

Wisconsin Decoy Collectors
Oshkosh, Wisconsin
Contact: Bill Brauer
Telephone: 414-921-2711

The West

Pacific Flyway Decoy Association
San Francisco and Sacramento, California
Contact: Sue Nesbit
P.O. Box 536, Quincy, CA 95971

West Coast Decoy Collectors Association
San Francisco, California
Contact: Hugh Chatham
Telephone: 415-621-1934

Museums

The following is a cross section of the continent's public repositories of carved waterfowl. Dozens of museums, historical societies and waterfowl refuges are the current homes of authentic working decoys of yesteryear, notable miniatures and decoratives by many of those same carvers, and contemporary birds by celebrated artisans of today.

It is suggested that collectors visit as many public and private accumulations as possible to look, ask questions, and learn a little more. In some situations with some curators, collectors may be able to hold and personally examine various pieces of particular collections. This is invaluable experience! With permission, you may also take photographs and may be able to purchase illustrated museum publications.

To that end, we have compiled an extensive, wide-ranging list of public institutions with the hope that their curators will see each and every one of you soon. Not all museum collections are on display at any given time; they may be in storage. Write or call before visiting; special arrangements when necessary can often be made. We invite any institution or individual to update or add to this inventory by sending information to us (see the Introduction for our address).

It should be noted that museums actively exhibiting and promoting decoys would greatly appreciate it if collectors would consider them for loan exhibitions and donations of a few birds or entire collections.

The Northeast

Boston Museum of Fine Arts, 465 Huntington Avenue, Boston, Massachusetts, 02115 (617-267-9300). Open year-round. The museum's collection of approximately forty decoys is mainly northeastern in origin. It includes a merganser by Captain Ben Smith, black duck by Benjamin Holmes, two sickle-bill curlews by William McMorrow, and others by Elisha Burr, W. J. Mathews, Levi Ellis, Joseph Walker, Albert Laing and George Boyd. Part of the

collection is usually on view. Contact the curator of American Decorative Arts.

Canadian Museum of Civilization, 1100 Laurier Street, P.O. Box 3100, Station B, Hull, Quebec, G8X 4H2 (819-776-7000). Open year-round. The museum has actively sought to become the national repository of Canadian decoys from all provenances and today houses over 1,000 lures from early Indian through 20th-century carvers. The collection has waterfowl lures not seen anywhere else. Contact the curator.

Cape Cod Museum of Natural History, P.O. Box 1710, Route 6A, Brewster, Massachusetts, 02631 (508-896-3867). Open year-round. Each September, the museum hosts its annual Bird Carvers Festival, a nationally recognized event which attracts international artists for a sale and competition. An auction is another feature of the event. Contact Dottie Thomas.

Connecticut River Foundation at Steamboat Dock, Inc., Foot of Main Street, Essex, Connecticut, 06426 (203-767-1564).

Dukes County Historical Society, Box 827, Cooke and School Street, Edgartown, Massachusetts, 02539 (508-627-4441). Open year-round. The society's collection consists entirely of Martha's Vineyard-related decoys (except for a few Mason Factory birds) with thirty-five working decoys, three miniatures, and a number of patterns used by Henry Keyes Chadwick. Nine hunting birds are by Chadwick, five by A. Elmer Crowell, two by Benjamin Smith (Chadwick's teacher); and one each by Winthrop Norton, Captain Robert Jackson, Frank Richardson and Manuel Swartz Roberts. Twelve local but unknowns are included. Some are on exhibit. Contact Director Marian Halperin.

Grafton Historical Society, Main Street, Grafton, Vermont, 05146 (802-843-2388). Open Memorial weekend through October 18. The collection was donated by Thomas Mellon Evans, Jr., an avid sportsman and collector of American antiques. It includes thirty-one examples made by the Mason Factory including perhaps the only known Mason Swan, thirteen by the Ward Brothers made between 1917 and 1966, and several dozen more by various east coast, midwest and Ontario carvers. There are a few decorative carvings. Contact Mrs. Jean L. Whitnack, curator.

McCord Museum of Canadian History, 690 Sherbrooke Street, West Montreal, Quebec, Canada, H3A 1E9 (514-398-7100). The collection presently contains over sixty-five working decoys primarily used in the province of Quebec, but other areas of eastern Canada are also represented. Signed examples by Orel LeBoeuf and other Montreal area carvers are included. There are, as well, about one dozen miniature decoys made during the first half of the twentieth century in eastern Canada. Several dozen native and folk carvings of waterfowl are part of the permanent collection that represent the carving traditions of Quebec. Decoys are occasionally on display in a changing exhibition program. Appointments to see the reserves may be made by writing the curatorial department or Marie Claire Morin, director of Development and Communications.

Maine State Museum, State House, LMA Building, Station 83, Augusta, Maine, 04333-0083 (207-289-2301). Open year-round. The majority of the museum's decoys are those which were either made or used in the state. Some of the Maine carvers represented are: Herbert A. Arey, Warren Billings, Lyford Coombs, Derwood, Maurice W. Ledbetter, Ben Gustafson and Carl Malmstrom of Vinalhaven; Lawrence Westom and G. Wimchembaugh of South Waldoboro; Gus Wilson of South Portland; Gordon Simmons of Pleasant Island; John Whitney of Falmouth; Ed Gammage of South Bristol; Ralph Hatch of Camden; Kendrick Doughty of Yarmouth; and George Huey of Friendship. There are no miniatures or decoratives. Decoys are not always on exhibit but are available for research by appointment. Contact the curator.

Museum of Fine Arts (Boston), 465 Huntington Avenue, Boston, Massachusetts, 02115 (617-267-9300). Open year-round. The museum possesses nearly forty working waterfowl, shorebirds and miniatures. The collection includes a pair of black ducks by Charles Hart; a redhead drake and hen, lesser scaup hen and black duck by Elmer Crowell; a black-breasted plover and winter yellowleg curlew by Elisha Burr; a golden plover by William J. Matthews; and black ducks by Albert Laing and Benjamin Holmes. There are a number of birds by anonymous makers from New England and the mid-Atlantic states, with attributions to such makers as George E. Boyd of New Hampshire (a canvas Canada goose) and John Williams of North Carolina (a whistling swan).

The collection was built in the 1950s and 1960s through the generosity and energy of Maxim Karolik, a great benefactor. Museum files indicate that Karolik and the curator of Decorative Arts at the Museum were in continuous contact with Dr. George Ross Starr and William J. Mackey, Jr. during this period. Several of the decoys now in the Museum's collection were previously owned by these famous collectors. One-third to one-half of the decoys are continuously on display using a rotating system. Contact the curator of American Decorative Arts.

Peabody Museum of Salem, East Indian Square, Salem, Massachusetts, 01970 (617-745-1876). Open year-round. Founded in 1799 by ship captains, the Peabody Museum is the oldest continuously operating museum in the United States. It has over 200 *working* decoys primarily from Massachusetts featuring carvings by Elmer Crowell, Joseph Lincoln, Keyes Chadwick, Captain Samuel Fabens, Stephen Badlam, Arthur Bamford, and Charles Hart, as well as other knowns and unknowns.

Carvers represented from other regions include a great Mason curlew, an Augustus Wilson over-sized turned-head goldeneye, a George Boyd yellowlegs and a pair of unknown eiders from Vinalhaven, Maine. Works are acquired through individual gifts and purchases with funds through the sale of expired Massachusetts waterfowl stamps. There are some decoratives by carvers such as Crowell and Hart (both deceased) and Captain Gerald Smith of Marblehead. Miniatures are by Elmer Crowell, Joseph Lincoln and A. J. King.

Every year from mid-September until Columbus Day the Peabody exhibits paintings of Massachusetts decoys. Contact Rob Moir, curator of natural history and Jackson Parker, honorary curator of waterfowl decoys.

Shelburne Museum, Route 7, Shelburne, Vermont, 05482 (802-985-3346). Open mid-May until mid-October. The nucleus of the Shelburne's massive grouping is the complete collection of Joel Barber, known as the "father of decoy collecting" and author of *Wild Fowl Decoys*. Later acquisitions from several other early collections added further strength. For many years, the strong curatorial hand of Robert Shaw has refined the massive collection of nearly 1,000 waterfowl carvings. The collection includes working decoys from every gunning region in North America and represents most all the major carvers. They also have over 200 miniature and decorative carvings as well as hunting paraphernalia, guns, boats, paintings, prints (including many Audubon engravings) and drawings. The collection is housed in the 1840 Dorset House, a charming Greek Revival-style farmhouse moved to the Museum from southern Vermont in 1953. The majority of the collection is on permanent exhibition. A "must" visit for any serious collector! Contact Curator Robert Shaw.

Stonington Historical Society, P.O. Box 103, Stonington, Connecticut, 06378 (203-535-8441). The Society has a collection of thirty to forty decoys. Contact the director.

Wendell Gilley Museum, Main Street and Herrick Road, P.O. Box 254, Southwest Harbor, Maine, 04679 (207-244-7555). Open May through December, closed on Mondays and holidays. The carving collections consist of works by Maine artist Wendell Gilley (1904–1983). A pioneer in the field of decorative bird carving and author of one of the first how-to books, *The Art of Bird Carving: A Guide to a Fascinating Hobby*, Gilley began carving miniatures in 1930, then expanded his work to include large scale decoratives, including life-size wild turkeys, bald eagles and great horned owls. Gilley also made a few working decoys for his personal use; they include white-wing, surf and common scoters, common eiders, a black duck, and yellowlegs. Original patterns, workbenches, tools, letters and memorabilia are also housed by the museum. Temporary exhibits of works by historical and contemporary carvers and other wildlife artists are offered as are decoy and decorative carving workshops, a

reference library, and taxidermy collection. Contact Nina Gormley, director/curator.

The Mid-Atlantic

Cape May Historical Museum, Cape May Court House, Route 9, New Jersey, 08210 (609-465-3535).

Museum of American Folk Art, Two Lincoln Square (Columbus Avenue between 65th and 66th Streets) New York, New York, 10023-6214 (212-595-9533). Open year-round. The museum has extensive holdings of almost 200 waterfowl decoys featuring many named makers who worked from the late nineteenth century through the mid-twentieth century along the Atlantic coast. Decoys made and used in Massachusetts are particularly well represented. An exhibition of over fifty decoys, accompanied by a full-color catalogue, toured nationally for three years. Selections from the collection are on view at various times. Serious researchers can contact Ralph Sessions, chief curator and Ann Marie Reilly, registrar.

Museums at Stony Brook, 1208 Route 25A, Stony Brook, New York, 11790. (516-751-0066). Open year-round. The collection includes 232 working decoys, the majority of which represent Long Island carvers and/or use. There are examples from other regions to put the Long Island decoys into a national context. Major carvers include Bill Bowman, Obediah Verity and Thomas Gelston. The collection began with generous donations by the Herrick family in the 1960s. Also in the 1960s, the museums acquired, through donation and purchase, a large collection from Robert Staniford. The museums continue to collect and actively pursue decoys which would round out the collection. The decoys are permanently exhibited in an interpretive gallery and adjoining study storage space. There are no miniatures or decoratives. Contact the director.

Noyes Museum, Lily Lake Road, Oceanville, New Jersey, 08231 (609-652-8848). Open year-round except national holidays and the week between Christmas and New Year's. The collection contains 300 to 400 decoys, most of which are working decoys from southern New Jersey carved between 1880 and 1925. Examples are: approximately 200 greater scaup by various carvers; shorebirds by H. V. Shourds and Daniel Lake Leeds; hunting rig of shorebird decoys by H. Boice circa 1880;

mergansers, black ducks, redheads, broadbills, goldeneyes, brant, geese and canvasbacks by Sam Soper, Henry Grant, H. V. Shourds, Mitchell Shourds, Daniel Lake Leeds, E. Hendrickson, Ward Brothers, Cobb family, Verity family, William Bowman, John Dilly, Mason Factory and others. There are a few contemporary carvings. A portion of the collection is on view at all times. Contact Gary Giberson.

Sayville Historical Society, Sayville, New York, 11782 (516-563-0186).

Staten Island Historical Society, Staten Island, New York, 10306 (718-351-1611). The society has a few dozen decoys kept in storage. Contact Maxine Friedman, chief curator.

Suffolk County Marine Museum, Sayville, New York, 11782 (516-567-1746).

1000 Islands Museum, 401 Riverside Drive, Old Town Hall, Clayton, New York, 12624 (315-686-5794). Open Memorial Day to Labor Day. Houses a fine collection of historic and decorative decoys and miniatures by many known makers. On exhibit. Contact Don Abbott.

The Central Atlantic

Abby Aldrich Rockefeller Folk Art Center, 307 S. England Street, P.O. Box C, Williamsburg, Virginia, 23187 (804-229-1000). Open year-round. Complementing the museum's American folk art emphasis are several dozen waterfowl from various hunting regions. Among the famous carvers whose works are in the museum are George Boyd, Charles Perdew, Charles Wheeler, Herman Glick, Roswell Bliss, Louis Hahn, Bert Graves and Joseph Sieger. Contact the curator.

Calvert Marine Museum, P.O. Box 97, Route 2, Solomons, Maryland, 20688 (301-326-2042). Open year-round except holidays. Amid their maritime historical artifacts of the Chesapeake, the museum has over forty decoys from the Susquehanna River and New England areas, as well as birds from the L. L. Bean and Wildflower companies. Carvers represented include the Ward Brothers, Hamilton Trossback, Madison Mitchell and Jess Urie. Contact the curator.

Chesapeake Bay Maritime Museum, P.O. Box 636, Mill Street, Navy Point, St. Michaels, Maryland,

21663 (301-745-2916). Open year-round. The museum has a very large collection of working decoys from private donations (including many from the carvers themselves) as well as purchases. The entire Chesapeake Bay region, eastern and western shores of Maryland and Virginia, form the majority of the collection with decoys by many of the well-documented makers. There are some miniatures and decoratives. Approximately 100 are on display at all times. Another exhibit area houses a rotating display of borrowed private collections on a wide range of subject matter. This changes four times a year. Contact the curator.

Chincoteague National Wildlife Refuge, P.O. Box 62, Chincoteague, Virginia, 23336 (804-336-6122). Open year-round. The historic collection includes a wide variety of decoys, guns, boats, and other hunting equipment. The collection was assembled over many years and features decoys from such famous eastern shore and Chincoteague carvers as Miles Hancock, Ira Hudson, Doug Jester and others. Primary contributors to the collection include Dr. Harry Walsh, Vernon Berg, Jr., and William Purnell, Jr. Parts of the collection are loaned to educational institutions such as the Ward Museum of Wildlife Art and the Smithsonian Institution on either long or short term loans. The collection is not currently open to the public; parts are used as demonstration models for interpretive programs featuring the history of waterfowling on Assateague Island. These programs are offered throughout the summer months and during the refuge Waterfowl Week celebration (from the Saturday before until the Sunday after Thanksgiving). Contact the refuge manager.

Eastern Shore of Virginia National Wildlife Refuge, R.F.D. #1, Box 122 B, Cape Charles, Virginia, 23310 (804-331-2760).

Havre de Grace Decoy Museum, P.O. Box A, Giles and Market Streets, Havre de Grace, Maryland, 21078 (301-939-3739). Open year-round except major holidays. The museum was formed to highlight the illustrious carvers of the Susquehanna Flats, and contains a very large collection of approximately 600 working decoys primarily from the Upper Chesapeake Bay region. Carvers such as Bob Litzenberg, Madison Mitchell, Charles "Speed" Joiner, Charles Bryan, Roger Urie and Jim Pierce are prominent. Numerous private collections contribute to their 276 miniatures. There are less than two dozen decoratives. Most of the collection is on display. The staff is developing interpretive permanent exhibits which will soon be available to the public after 1992. Contact the director.

Maryland Historical Society, 201 W. Monument St., Baltimore, Maryland, 21201 (301-685-3750). The society houses a small collection of decoys donated from several collectors as well as a maritime collection. Contact the director.

Refuge Waterfowl Museum, P.O. Box 272, Maddox Boulevard, Chincoteague, Virginia, 23336 (804-336-5800). Open daily spring and summer; weekends fall and winter. In the late 1970s John Maddox built the museum to house a collection of several thousand decoys. There are working decoys and decoratives. Atlantic Flyway carvers are in the majority and include Ira Hudson, Doug Jester, Elmer Crowell, Lee Dudley and Cobb Island carvers. Birds from other flyways are present. Contact John Maddox.

Smithsonian Institution, 1000 Jefferson Drive, SW, Washington, District of Columbia, 20560 (202-357-1771). Open year-round. The National Museum of American Art contains a few decoys which were part of the Herbert Hemphill folk art collection acquired in the 1980s. There is an attributed Roger Williams, a John McLaughlin, a Wilbur Corwin and several other unidentified working decoys. There are no decoratives or miniatures. Contact Andrew Connors or Linda Hartigan.

The National Museum of the American Indian, a part of the Smithsonian, is presently headquartered in New York City. (They will move to new space in Washington D.C. in the early 1990s.) They have the Indian decoys discovered in Lovelock Cave, Nevada, in 1923. Contact the curatorial offices at 212-828-6969.

Upper Bay Museum, 219 Walnut Street, P.O. Box 11275, North East, Maryland, 21901 (301-287-5718). Open Memorial Day until October; winter months by appointment. The museum houses over 800 working and decorative carvings, the majority by carvers of the upper shore of the Chesapeake such as Wally Algard, George Barnes, Samuel Barnes, Taylor Boyd, Joseph Coudon, James Currier, Ben Dye, Paul Gibson, William Heveren, John

"Daddy" Holly, Bob Litzenburg, Bob McGaw, Jim Pierce, Ira Hudson, Amos Waterfield and many more. The work of Madison Mitchell is highlighted. Contact Stanley M. White.

Virginia Marine Science Museum, 717 General Booth Boulevard, Virginia Beach, Virginia, 32451 (804-425-3476). Open year-round. The museum features working decoys and contemporary carvings from Back Bay and Currituck. Historic makers represented include Lee Dudley, Ned Burgess, Mannie Heywood, Bob Morse, Ivy Stevens, John Williams, and Alvirah Wright. Since its opening in 1986, the museum has held exhibitions under the auspices of the Back Bay Wildfowl Guild. Twice a year decoys from the museum are augmented with examples from carvers and collectors to produce new perspectives. Contact Mark Swingle.

Ward Museum of Wildfowl Art, Beaglin Park Road & South Schumaker Drive, P.O. Box 3416, Salisbury, Maryland, 21802 (301-742-4586). Open year-round. New museum quarters to open in the Spring of 1992 with an inaugural exhibit and many activities. In 1968 a group of Salisbury businessmen and decoy collectors feared that the traditional art of decoy making would soon be supplanted by mass-produced plastic versions. These leaders started the organization to promote the art and craft of decoy carving and to establish a forum for carving competitions and the exhibition of wildfowl art. (The organization was named in honor of Steve and Lemuel Ward, two highly regarded decoy makers from Crisfield, Maryland.)

Over the next twenty years, they accumulated 175 decoys and other art work carved by the Ward Brothers, 200 antique decoys, sixty transitional carvings dating from 1950 to 1970, 350 contemporary carvings of all types, forty antique hunting artifacts, 120 antique carving tools, 200 miniature carvings and forty-five paintings and prints. They began what is generally regarded as the oldest annual wildfowl art exhibition, held each October. In 1971 the Ward Foundation World Championship Wildfowl Carving Competition was established as a means of raising carving standards and building in one place a collection of examples from the very best contemporary carvers.

In the Spring of 1992, the newly-built museum will open. It is situated on a four acre site (a gift from the City of Salisbury) alongside a pond with both marsh and woodland frontage. The inaugural exhibition will be an astounding display of museum and privately owned wildfowl carvings and art. The facilities are designed as a teaching institution. Another "must" visit for collectors and carvers. Exhibits and educational programs will be available all year. Contact the curators.

The South

Dallas Museum of Natural History, P.O. Box 26193, Dallas, Texas, 75226 (214-421-2169). Open year-round except Christmas. The museum's thirty-two working decoys are part of a larger offering of more than 500 species of Texas bird specimens, many of them in the Habitat Galleries. The antique decoys are from several hunting areas and include some factory lures. Ira Hudson, Doug Jester, Perry Wilcox and Lloyd Tyler are a few of the carvers represented. Contact the curator of ornithology.

Louisiana State Museum, 751 Chartres St., New Orleans, Louisiana, 70116 (504-568-6968). Open year-round except major holidays. The focus of the museum is the history of the Baton Rouge area. Twenty of Louisiana's working decoys dating from the late 19th century through 1940 are on display. Some of the decoys are vintage lures and then donated to the museum by author/historian Charles Frank. The balance are prize-winning waterfowl carvings from annual competitions held by the Louisiana Duck Carvers and Collectors Guild. Collection is not currently on exhibition. Call or write the curator in advance for an appointment to see the decoys.

North Carolina Maritime Museum, 315 Front St., Beaufort, North Carolina, 28516 (919-728-7317). Open year-round except holidays. The museum houses over 100 decoys mostly made by southern decoy carvers, the majority from the James Lewis collection. Some of these were made by Ivey Stevens, Mannie Haywood, Ned Burgess, Wilbur Simpson, Ammie Paul, Mitchel Fulcher and Emmet White. The collection is in storage when special exhibits of private collections are on view; otherwise, at least half the museum collection is on display. Contact Connie Mason, collections manager.

West Baton Rouge Museum, 845 North Jefferson Avenue, Port Allen, Louisiana, 70767 (504-336-2422). Open year-round. The Museum's collection of about twenty working decoys, except two, was a gift of Durbin Benjamin Kleinpeter of Baton Rouge. All the birds were made by such famous Louisiana carvers as Domingo Campo, Mark McCool Whipple, Xavier Bourg, Alcide Cormardelle, Clovis "Cadise" Vizier, George Frederick, Reme Roussell, Dewey Pertuit, Laurent Verdin and Samson Foret. There are one or two decoratives and no miniatures. Contact the curator of decoys.

Zigler Museum, 411 Clara St., Jennings, Louisiana, 70546 (318-824-0114). Open year-round. The museum purchased the decorative Best in Show carvings at the 1984, 1985 and 1987 Louisiana Wildfowl Carvers and Collectors Guild competition. They are: two ring-neck ducks by Michael Bonner of New Orleans (1984), two wood ducks by Ivan Boudier of Lafayette (1985), and a blue- wing teal by Jimmy Toups of Schriever (1987). They also have three donated cypress working decoys. Contact Director Dolores Spears.

The Midwest

Art Institute of Chicago, Michigan Avenue & Adams, Chicago, Illinois, 60603 (312-443-3645). Open year-round. The institute has a small collection of Illinois River decoys. Contact Milo Naeve, curator, Department of American Arts.

Backus Conservation Education Centre, (located at Backus Heritage Conservation Area, Port Rowan, Ontario), c/o Long Point Region Conservation Authority, R.R. #3, Simcoe, Ontario, Canada, N3Y 4K2 (519-428-4623). Open year-round. The majority of the decoys are on indefinite loan from the Canadian Wildlife Service. Approximately twenty decoys date from the late 1800s to early 1900s with a number of Phineas Reeves. Several dozen Long Point area decoys, primarily from the Long Point Company, have recently been donated as a highlight of several displays in the new wildfowling exhibit gallery. No miniatures. One Max Chute decorative killdeer. Most are on permanent display. Contact Janice Robertson, supervisor of community relations.

Chicago Historical Society, Clark Street at North Avenue, Chicago, Illinois, 60614 (312-642-4600). Open year-round. The collection of twenty-five midwest decoys was donated in 1971 by Ralph M.

Loeff. Carvers from Illinois, Michigan, Minnesota, Wisconsin and Iowa make up the grouping which includes Leonard Doren, Charles Perdew, Bert Graves, Henry Holmes, Hector Whittington, Russell McKaufsky, Virgil Lashbrook, Fred J. Ellis, Jim Robar, Louis P. Kelley, Ed "One-Arm" Kellie, Ben Schmidt and several factories. The collection has been on exhibit in the past. Contact the Department of Decorative and Industrial Arts.

Cincinnati Museum of Natural History, Frederick and Amey Geier Collections and Research Center, 1720 Gilbert Avenue, Cincinnati, Ohio, 45202 (513-621-3890). Open year-round. There are a total of eighty-six pieces, most of which are miniatures and decoratives by Elmer Crowell of East Harwich, Massachusetts. The collection was originally owned by Stephen Arthur Gould and later donated to the museum by Charles Fleischmann. Interestingly, the Cincinnati Museum, which opened its doors in 1818, once employed the famed artist and naturalist John James Audubon to gather and mount a collection of fauna. The museum's direction and Audubon's influence is felt in their collections today. The Crowell collection is complemented by the rare, complete sets of Federal Migratory Waterfowl Stamps and Prints as well as over ninety original watercolor paintings of waterfowl by Robert Verity Clem of Chatham, Massachusetts.

The museum hosted an exhibition entitled "Against the Grain: One Hundred Years of the Bird Carver's Art" in 1983. DeVere Burt wrote in *Ward Foundation News*: "Thus, against the backdrop of Crowell's magnificent miniatures, is displayed the work of Contemporary carvers who were invited to exhibit alongside the master. Selected carvers include: Don Briddell, Mt. Airy, Maryland, Dr. H. S. Doolittle, Jr., Darien, Connecticut; W. Craig Hellmers, Pekin, Illinois; Glenn D. Ormsby, Smithfield, Virginia; Jim Sprankle, Annapolis, Maryland; and Dr. Mark Taddonio, York, Pennsylvania. All of these men have achieved some success at the prestigious Ward Foundation World Championship Wildfowl Carving Competition in recent years.

"Four regional carvers also exhibit to provide a local focus on the craft. Included are: Gary Denzler, Cincinnati, Ohio; Robert Hawkins, Cincinnati, Ohio; Dr. M. J. Minarcheck, Bethell, Ohio; and David Monhollen, Union, Kentucky. The work of the contemporary carvers contrasts dramatically with the Crowell pieces and clearly demonstrates the evolution of design and sophistication of technique embodied in the beautiful work of successful modern carvers." The collection is held in storage except for an occasional exhibition. Contact Beth Merritt, collections manager.

Cleveland Museum of Natural History, 1 Wade Oval, University Circle, Cleveland, Ohio, 44106-1767 (216-231-4600). Open year-round. In the 1960s the museum acquired, through purchase and gifts, the decoys of Albert Dixon Simmons. These comprise most of the sizeable collection today. The Atlantic and Mississippi flyways are represented by many well-published carvers and factories. In 1979 the museum presented a stylishly-designed and cataloged exhibition highlighting decoys from their collection as well as from private collectors. Decoys are usually in storage but upon request and approval are lent to appropriate institutions or organizations. Contact Curator Ellen Walters and Registrar Carole Camillo.

Crane Creek Wildlife Experiment Station, Crane Creek State Park, Oak Harbor, Ohio (on Route 2 between Sandusky and Toledo) (419-898-0960). The Station houses and displays several hundred decoys used on Lake Erie and its adjoining marshes. Many Michigan, Ohio and Ontario lures are exhibited by known and unknown makers. Contact the manager.

Delta Museum and Archives, 4858 Delta Street, Delta, British Columbia, Canada, V4K 2T8. (604-946-9322 or 946-6262). Open year-round. The archives houses seven working decoys by carvers Allard Waddell, Jack Jameson, J. Mason and True H. Oliver and some related material as well. Contact Director Leigh Hussey.

Eva Brook Donly Museum, 109 Norfolk St., Simcoe, Ontario, Canada, N3Y 2W3 (519-426-1583). Open year-round. The collection contains approximately sixty items at present. The most interesting are some twenty-five older decoys from the Long Point area, most donated by The Long Point Company and the company's keeper, Mr. Buck Wamsley. These are working decoys used on Long Point Company lands, many with brands and initials of owners who were members of that famed hunting club. Condition varies. A variety of species are represented dating from about 1870 to about 1940. Other working decoys are generally later and from lesser-known carvers and amateur carver/hunters of the Norfolk County area (circa 1900 to 1960) such as: Ernie Post, Ernie Castleton, William Shaver, Robert McCairns, Lee Hodges and Walter Bailey. There are three decoys by Ken Anger of Dunnville—one from his early period. A special rarity is a circa 1870 painted tin silhouette attributed to one of a small number of decoys by Phineas Reeves of Long Point. There are ten miniatures by Bev Kett made between 1973 and 1979 and a contemporary canvasback made in 1986 by Dennis Runge, of Long Point. Most of the collection is in storage, but about twenty to twenty-five are on long term exhibit in the museum's main gallery. Others are rotated from time to time. Contact the curator.

Greenfield Village and Henry Ford Museum, Oakwood Boulevard, Dearborn, Michigan, 48121 (313-271-1620, ext. 589). Open year-round. The museum has several hundred working decoys in their extensive Americana collections. They are usually in storage (except for special exhibits) and can be seen by appointment. Contact Donna Braden.

Illinois State Museum, Corner Spring and Edward Sts., Springfield, Illinois, 62706 (217-782-7386). Open year-round except Easter, Thanksgiving, Christmas and New Year's Day. The museum has a collection of over 170 Illinois River Valley decoys including such carvers as Robert Elliston, Otto Garren, Charles Heppner, Henry Holmes, Fred Mott, George Pensinger and Charles Perdew. Many were donated by Joseph French. Five decoys will be on permanent display in an exhibition in May of 1992. The rest are occasionally featured in special exhibits. Researchers may contact the Decorative Arts department.

Kortright Centre, c/o Metro Conservation Authority, 5 Shorthand Drive, Downsview, Ontario, Canada, M3N 1S4 (416-832-2289). Located north of Toronto, they do not have a permanent display of decoys, but hold excellent waterfowl exhibits on occasion. Contact the director.

Lakeview Museum of Arts and Sciences, 1125 West Lake Avenue, Peoria, Illinois, 61614 (309-686-7000). Open year-round. The museum has a small but growing collection of Illinois River working decoys which includes several fine Charles Perdew, Bert Graves, and other Peoria area decoys. A serious collection was initiated in the late 1980s and is developing primarily through gifts and bequests, supplemented by contributions for purchases. Two large loan exhibitions were held during the 1980s featuring the best of the Illinois River decoys. They have no miniatures at present. A small portion of the collection is usually on exhibit. Contact Museum Director Michael Sanden.

Leigh Yawkey Woodson Art Museum, 700 North 12th Street, Wausau, Wisconsin, 54401 (715-845-7010). Open year-round. The museum has a small collection of historic working decoys. These include a pair of mallards circa 1925 by the Armstrong Feather Company of St. Louis, Missouri. There are also a pair of bluebills carved circa 1932 by David Paul Bierbauer of Wausau, a canvasback by Harry Croy, and an American goldeneye by John Nierman, all of Wisconsin.

The permanent collection also contains over thirty decorative bird sculptures. They were created by nationally and internationally acclaimed carvers such as John Sheeler, Larry Barth, Marcus Schultz, Robert Guge, Dick LeMaster, Ernie Muehlmatt, Charles Greenough Chase, John Sharp, Leo and Lee Osborne and Van Keuren Marshall to name a few. Each fall the museum organizes an exhibition entitled "Birds in Art" which includes approximately 120 works of art featuring birds as the primary or secondary focus. As many as one-quarter of these works are sculptures of birds in bronze, stone, and welded steel as well as painted and unpainted wood carvings. The exhibition, which opens the weekend following Labor Day and runs through late October, includes artists from all over the world. Contact Andrew J. McGivern, curator of exhibitions.

Michigan State University, Kresge Art Gallery, West Circle Drive, East Lansing, Michigan, 48824-2370 (517-355-2370). Open year-round. The museum displays periodic exhibitions of Michigan carved decoys and its waterfowling traditions. There are collections of hunting, fishing and trapping equipment (duck boats, blinds and decoys) from the state. Historical documents were donated from the Phyllis Ellison collection. Contact Dr. C. Kurt Dewhurst, director, or Dr. Marsha MacDowell, curator of folk arts.

Milwaukee Public Museum, 800 W. Wells St., Milwaukee, Wisconsin, 53233 (414-278-2700). Open year-round. The museum houses a nice collection of over 200 working and decorative decoys from the eastern and Mississippi flyways. Some of the carvers represented are: Ben Holmes, Shang Wheeler, Chris Powers, Charles Perdew, Charles Walker, Catherine and Robert Elliston and Hector Whittington. Factories include Mason Decoy Company, Tru Dux, and Pratt Manufacturing Company. Of special interest are decoys designed by Owen Gromme. By appointment only. Contact John Lundstrom, curator (414-278-2794).

Missouri Historical Society, Lindell & DeBaliviere, St. Louis, Missouri, 63112 (314-361-1424). Open year-round. There are just three decoys in the collection. One is known to date to around 1860 and another to circa 1900. The museum has not had them identified as yet. All are currently in storage. Contact the director of museum collections.

Oshkosh Public Museum, 1331 Algoma Boulevard, Oskosh, Wisconsin, 54901 (414-424-0452). Open year-round. All working decoys represent carvers of the Winnebago Lakes region of Wisconsin and span the years 1870 to 1940. Decoys were made by Frank Resop, Paul Doering, Frank Strey, August Nelow, August Moak and others. Parts of the collection may be on exhibit at any time. The museum mounted a major exhibit in 1989. Contact the chief curator or director.

The West

Denver Museum of Natural History, 2001 Colorado Boulevard, Denver, Colorado, 80205 (303-370-6357). Open year-round. The museum exhibits The Douglas E. Miller Carved Bird Collection. It includes antique decoys as well as decoratives by such artists as Larry Hayden, W. L. Schultz, Roger Barton, Ron Tepley, and John Sheeler. Contact Betsy Webb.

Los Angeles County Natural History Museum, 900 Exposition Boulevard, Los Angeles, California, 70009 (213-744-3366). Open year-round except Christmas day. The Birds and Mammals Section of the museum has twenty-five working decoys and nearly seventy-five decorative wildfowl carvings donated by Douglas E. Miller. Artists include Roger Barton, Larry Hayden, Pat Godin, Robert Kerr, C.W. Miller, Charles Wargo, Bruce Burke, Jack Franco and others. The birds are on display. Contact Kimball Garrett.

Las Vegas Natural History Museum, 900 Las Vegas Boulevard, North, Las Vegas, Nevada, 89132 (702-384-3466). Open year-round. Exhibits the Douglas E. Miller collection which includes hundreds of working and decorative decoys and wildfowl. Two to three-hundred carvings are on display at all times; others in storage. Contact Marilyn Gillipse.

National Carvers Museum, 14960 Woodcarver Road, Monument, Colorado, 80132 (303-481-2656). Open year-round except holidays. The museum was formed in 1969 for the exhibition of woodcarvings. They have around 9,000 works from the huge membership of the National Carvers Museum Foundation. One-hundred decoys and decoratives are on exhibit. Contact Public Information.

San Francisco Bay National Wildlife Refuge, P.O. Box 524, (off Route 237) Newark, California, 94560 (415-792-0222). Open year-round except holidays. The wildlife refuge houses a small collection of decorative bird carvings by Nancy Lyons. Exhibited are mallards, ruddy ducks, surf scoter, bufflehead, canvasback and other species. Contact the refuge assistant.

Photo Credits

Our heartfelt thanks to every photographer who loaned his work to this project.

David Allen (Richard W. Oliver Auction Gallery)

Dave and Mary Ahrendt

Roger Barton

David Beane (James Julia/Gary Guyette, Inc.)

Marc Bernsau (Richard W. Oliver Auction Gallery)

Vickie Briddell, Maryland

Ken Burris (Shelburne Museum)

Bruce Cameron

Mike Conover, Winfield, Kansas

Doyle Auction Gallery

Thomas Eckert

Charles Frank

Bernie Gates

Pat Godin

Gary Guyette

Ted Harmon

Everette James

Gene Kangas

William J. Koelpin

Allan Lieberman (Richard Bourne Company, Inc.)

Dick McIntyre

Russ Marshall, Detroit, Michigan

Ellen Meserve (Richard W. Oliver Auction Gallery)

Thomas J. O'Connor III

Torrey Reily

Leo Osborne

John Root, Anacortes, Washington

Frank Schmidt

Dennis Schroeder

Ronald Sharp

Shelburne Museum

Peter Van Tright

Barton Walter

Ward Foundation

Bob White

Contributors

We want to thank each of these most gracious individuals and institutions for contributing their time, knowledge, information, ideas, decoys, and materials to this endeavour.

Dave and Mary Ahrendt
Ora Anderson
John Althans
The Cliff Avann Family
Jack Barrett
Roger Barton
Carol and Bill Bender
Don Briddell
Tan Brunet
Richard A. Bourne Company, Inc.
Bob Brown
Dick Brust
Alton Buchman
Bruce Cameron
James Campbell
Canadian Museum of Civilization
Richard Carlson
Don Cassini
Brian Cheramie
Cleveland Museum of Natural History
Jim Cook
Dean Dashner
Habbart Dean
Decoys Unlimited
Ed de Navarre
William Doyle Auction Gallery
Timothy Eastland
Thomas Eckert
Judy and Douglas Elliott
Phyllis Ellison
Oliver Emerson
Steve Fall
Henry Fleckenstein

Charles Frank
Ronald J. Gard
Bernie Gates
Pat Godin
Dale and Gary Guyette
Michael Hall
Walter Hallbauer
Ted Harmon
Charlie Hart
John Hillman
Roberta Holcomb
Everette James
James Julia/Gary Guyette, Inc.
Mark Kangas
William J. Koelpin
Jim Lancer
Bruce Malcolm
C. J. Marsolek
James McCleery
Nash McIntosh
Dick McIntyre, Collectable Old Decoys
Mr. and Mrs. Thomas O'Connor III
Richard W. Oliver Auction Gallery
Leo Osborne
Don Pawlaczyk
Art Philp
Private Collections
George Quay
Richard Riemenschneider
Torrey Reily
Frank Schmidt
Dennis Schroeder
Janet and Ron Sharp
John Sharp
Robert Shaw
Shelburne Museum
William Sherar

George Starr
Carol and E. C. Swift
William A. Taylor
Mike Thomas
George Thompson
William Towner
Peter Van Trigt

Barton Walter
Bud Ward
Bob White
Bruce Williams
Todd Wohlt
Bob Youngman

Index